"This volume is very much needed and long-awaited in the field of TESOL. I can't remember being as excited about a new book as much as I am about this one and look forward to adding it to my professional library."

—Christine Coombe
Associate Professor, Dubai Men's College, Dubai, United Arab Emirates, and
TESOL International Association President (2011–2012)

"England provides real ways for TESOLers to take control of their paths and position themselves to make the most of their talents. This book succeeds in empowering the individual, but its compound impact will undoubtedly raise the professionalism of the entire TESOL field."

—Jackie Gishbaugher
MA, doctoral student, University of Memphis, Memphis, TN, USA

"I highly recommend this book for novice teachers who do not want to experience burnout too soon in the job and for mid-career and experienced professionals who want to stay motivated and fulfilled. A much-needed book in our field!"

—Amira Salama
MA, American University in Cairo, Cairo, Egypt

"Regardless of the stage at which you are at as an English language teaching professional, you will benefit from reading this new book and gaining insights into how to take charge of your own professional development."

—Neil J. Anderson
Professor, Brigham Young University – Hawaii, Laie, HI, USA, and TESOL
International Association President (2001–2002)

TESOL CAREER PATH DEVELOPMENT

This book addresses a wide range of issues and obstacles that teachers in native and non-native English-speaking countries face in teaching English language learners of all ages, at all levels of proficiency, and in a variety of program settings. The book introduces a model of milestones for career path development specific to the specialized needs and skills of the TESOL (Teaching English to Speakers of Other Languages) community that caters to the many unique challenges faced by teachers at a range of experience levels, from preservice and novice teachers to veteran and semi-retired professionals.

Taking an interdisciplinary approach and drawing on the voices and experiences of TESOL scholars, England demonstrates how best to apply one's education, background, and experiences to individuals who work in the field of TESOL, and offers unique tools, strategies, and training techniques. This book provides a clear and engaging framework for scholars and teachers at any stage in one's career to grow and develop professionally in fast-changing and increasingly complex professional climates.

This book is ideal for scholars, graduate students, and researchers in TESOL and language teaching, as well as scholars and researchers in international teacher development and language teaching.

Liz England presents frequently on TESOL career development at TESOL conferences worldwide and has led both pre- and in-service professional development projects for language teachers in universities, public and private K-12 schools and workplace settings in the United States and worldwide. She was previously Professor and Chair of TESOL, School of Education and Human Development, Shenandoah University, Winchester, VA, USA.

TESOL CAREER PATH DEVELOPMENT

Creating Professional Success

Liz England

NEW YORK AND LONDON

First published 2020
by Routledge
52 Vanderbilt Avenue, New York, NY 10017

and by Routledge
2 Park Square, Milton Park, Abingdon, Oxon, OX14 4RN

Routledge is an imprint of the Taylor & Francis Group, an informa business

© 2020 Taylor & Francis

The right of Liz England to be identified as author of this work has been asserted by her in accordance with sections 77 and 78 of the Copyright, Designs and Patents Act 1988.

All rights reserved. No part of this book may be reprinted or reproduced or utilised in any form or by any electronic, mechanical, or other means, now known or hereafter invented, including photocopying and recording, or in any information storage or retrieval system, without permission in writing from the publishers.

Trademark notice: Product or corporate names may be trademarks or registered trademarks, and are used only for identification and explanation without intent to infringe.

Library of Congress Cataloging-in-Publication Data
A catalog record for this title has been requested

ISBN: 978-1-138-31205-0 (hbk)
ISBN: 978-1-138-31206-7 (pbk)
ISBN: 978-0-429-45848-4 (ebk)

Typeset in Bembo
by Cenveo® Publisher Services

 Printed in the United Kingdom
by Henry Ling Limited

This book is dedicated to inspiring teachers who've come into my life – in many roles, sometimes even as students – and taught me many important lessons. And here are the names of those who have taught me the most (and keep teaching me every day): my amazing son, Sam; my beloved grandmother, Nana, Mary Elizabeth Hill Harris; my extraordinary Aunt Peggy, Margaret Frances Harris Flower; and Professors Doug Brown, Sandy Savignon, Braj Kachru, Howard Maclay, Lyle Bachman, Muriel Saville-Troike, Said El Badawi, and Saad Gamal.

CONTENTS

List of figures	*x*
List of tables	*xi*
Acknowledgments	*xii*
1 Introduction	1
2 Theorizing TESOL Career Path Development	11
3 Teacher Education	30
4 Teacher Motivation	42
5 Organizational Development	50
6 Leadership	60
7 Life Balance	69
8 Rewards and Milestones	83
9 Moving Forward – Roles of Educational Organizations and Language Teachers Associations	94
10 It's On Us: Intentional TESOL Career Path Development	104
References	*112*
Index	*121*

FIGURES

2.1	Context of TESOL career path development	14
2.2	TESOL career path development	15
6.1	Cathy's career path	64

TABLES

2.1	Characteristics of English language teachers at five career path stages	25
6.1	Characteristics of TESOL leaders and leadership	65
7.1	Some strategies for English language teachers' life balance at five career stages	77
10.1	Advocacy skills for five career stages	109

ACKNOWLEDGMENTS

It took decades for me to come to the point in life to write this book. I am fortunate to have been able to have met, then worked with, thousands of teachers worldwide. All of them have touched me in some way. A small subset of nearly 50 of those teachers have become close friends, my TESOL family, and those whose encouragement and whose own stories along with my own have driven me to pursue this writing project. They know who they are and now, so do readers! While their names will remain theirs to reveal as they see fit in the future, I bow to and am very grateful to those who agreed to let me share their career path development experiences in this book. My thanks to Routledge Taylor & Francis editor, Karen Adler, who has tirelessly answered questions and gently nudged me forward on my first solo book. Thanks to Lisa Strimple, a devoted and careful assistant, for her help in getting the references right. And to the Shenandoah University Library logging quite literally hundreds of hours, and where I was the recipient of the competence and kindness of the professional staff librarians there. Heartfelt thanks go to my tribe – a small group of friends and colleagues inside and outside TESOL, near and mostly far (in person, on the phone, and on social media), who have read and commented on various pieces of the text. Finally, to the anonymous reviewers who provided clarity, honesty, and kindness in their invaluable comments and perspectives, I owe undying gratitude. Any weaknesses and all errors are mine alone; but without these individuals' love and efforts, this book would be less than it is here.

1

INTRODUCTION

Overview

In these times of attacks on education in general and teachers in particular in the United States and worldwide, we need to support professionalism in teaching. This book is designed to provide a tool for Teachers of English to Speakers of Other Languages (heretofore described as "TESOL") professionals who seek to build satisfying careers.

Why are TESOL career paths important to address now? With increasing changes in the world – economies, organizations, industries, and societal perspectives – the world of work is changing for us too. With increasing numbers of employable retirement-eligible people, larger numbers of single parent and both adults working households, and job options for working "remotely" or "from home," lifestyles are changing generally. And professional work lives are not what they used to be – one job for one's entire career. Increasingly nowadays, employers – schools, universities, and organizations – want to hire based on a portfolio of skills and knowledge both for the present and for the future needs of their clientele. TESOL professionals need to be thinking more strategically about their work lives with a focus on ways in which their skills and knowledge maximize their value for a school, university, or organization. The balance between the needs of employees and the needs of schools and other institutions is dramatically changing. Today's TESOL employment world means maximizing individual needs with organizational potential. The predictable straight-line to success and job satisfaction is no longer available to most of us.

One approach to this new way of looking at our work can be found in Carter, Cook, and Dorsey (2009), where five fundamental components of career path

2 Introduction

development (CPD) were identified (p. 4). While their analysis addresses industry, there is much to be learned for TESOLers in this list (adapted for TESOLers): (1) a sequential description of one's positions and roles, (2) educational qualifications (academic degrees) and licensure and/or certifications, (3) critical developmental experiences (formal training courses beyond those for educational, licensure, and/or certification above), (4) information about the strengthening of competencies, and (5) information about the importance of prospective employer's list of key factors. Other information may vary, depending on the context (salaries, growth rates, recruitment plans, etc.). In TESOL, we rarely hear this type of conversation. Instead, we focus squarely on the responsibilities of teachers to do a good job. A brief scan of recent TESOL International Association Conference programs or International Association of Teachers of English as a Foreign Language (IATEFL) programs reveal a strong emphasis on learners', not teachers' needs.

In fact, until now, the emphasis in TESOL professional excellence has been placed almost exclusively on learners – providing teachers with new ideas and research to improve the ways in which they deliver instruction. Programs, too, are the object of study as they address efforts to increase learners' speed and level of proficiency in learning English. Rarely do we see efforts to provide teachers with research-based tools for addressing satisfying careers. While acknowledging the value and importance of learners and programs in effective instruction, this book emphasizes the role of teachers and their value and importance. By focusing on a better and clearer understanding of what TESOL CPD actually is for teachers, we can understand and support teachers in new and better ways. This book is a first in doing that: establishing a research base for studying TESOL CPD and ultimately, providing tools for research, strong teacher education programs, and efforts to promote job satisfaction and instructional excellence.

Huberman (1993) describes the life of a teacher drawing heavily on Fessler (1985), who identifies what might be called psychological stages of teachers' career paths. And in addition, Huberman refers to Steffy and Wolfe (2001), who found six stages of teacher development, emphasizing the fact that these stages are not necessarily linear while describing findings including disengagement and teachers leaving the profession. While these findings are of interest and useful to those who want to study CPD among teachers in one specific geographic region, the teachers who were subjects in the research reported by Huberman, Fessler, and Steffy fit a different profile from those who are the focus of this book. Here, I focus squarely on teachers of English to speakers of other languages who work in many different countries worldwide. In addition, teachers described in this volume seek to remain in the profession, at least for as long as it is possible for them to do that. The forces that guide TESOLers along their career paths are different from those found in the aforementioned studies; and at times, those forces operate in complex, nonlinear ways.

Indeed, the research reported by Steffy and Wolfe (2001) reminds us of the fact that CPD is not a superficial experience for most TESOLers. Our career paths affect us deep down inside – our self-esteem, self-image, identity, values, and meaning. We experience a wide range of emotions as we move along. All career paths know ups and downs, promotions and downsizing, tenure decisions, making choices about work and home life, and dealing with successes and failures. We have fears, concerns, anxiety, self-doubt, disappointments, failures, rejection, criticism, and doubt from friends and even from our families. And for many, there can be incredible guilt attached to TESOL careers as we work long hours (sometimes in service to the profession and/or as volunteers) and for many, travel the world leaving sometimes sad and frightened family members and friends behind. My own mother literally planned the funeral of my son and me as we prepared to leave for Egypt in 1984. She phoned the funeral director in our small town: "Jimmy," she said, "I want to plan my daughter's funeral. She's going to Egypt." After a pause, Jimmy said, "Dorothy, she has to die first. Let's worry about her funeral when she's actually dead, OK?" I went to Egypt knowing that my mother thought I would die there – and I was taking her only grandson along with me too. A lot of guilt there!

And finally, consider the following brief story, familiar to many TESOLers and related here by a colleague: I remember all the times when I've said "I teach English as a second language" and get a return comment like "Oh, I was going to do that." Or "I was thinking about doing that for extra money" or "I'd like to try that – so I can travel!" – and my own cringing as if it were something one could just "do" – with no training, because one has the privilege of having been born as a native speaker of English. While the TESOL profession was established in 1966 with the founding of the TESOL International Association, still, today, in 2018, we face this ongoing misunderstanding among those who simply don't know we exist as an actual profession, containing an academic research canon, postgraduate educational requirements, and specific knowledge and skills. It is overdue for us to begin thinking more strategically about TESOL professional employment issues in general. In this book, we begin to do that by addressing teachers' career paths in our field.

In my experience (and that too perhaps of some readers), career paths and talent management have simply not gone together for TESOLers. The result is the too frequent reality of programs staffed by teachers who are untrained or undertrained and who secure jobs for reasons having little to do with their professional expertise nor their track record, teachers who enroll in and complete educational programs where there is little or no connection to or awareness of the real world of TESOL professional employment and sadly, teachers who become burntout, abused by employers, unprepared with the skills and credentials needed to obtain good jobs or working in programs where instruction is not a priority and teacher compensation is below standard.

4 Introduction

In the chapters that follow, I hope to offer a pathway for TESOLers to acquire knowledge, skills, and habits that will allow not just a few but all TESOLers to know the kind of joy, satisfaction, and sense of professional accomplishment I have personally been fortunate to have known.

I hope that in reading this book, English teachers worldwide will be asking themselves, their professional associations, and their employers for appropriate levels of investment in and prioritizing of funding so that training and development needs of teachers are adequately addressed to create opportunities for excellent instruction and professional satisfaction for teachers at all stages of their career paths.

At the same time, building a career in TESOL can be exciting and empowering. My own career, with a number of job changes, is one example. And I invite readers to consider their own TESOL careers – however long or short – as you anticipate moving ahead. Ours is a truly extraordinary field; and we have knowledge and skills of interest to other fields too. Consider your TESOL life – all of it – and read on.

In an effort to provide a starting point (and for some perhaps a model), here's an abbreviated autobiography. My career path has been guided by an exceptionally well-developed work ethic, honed in childhood as the first-born child and grandchild of my Scottish American mother and father and my grandparents too. Ours was a rich extended family environment filled with obligations and yes, some fun. No one in my family earned a doctoral degree or even a Master's. One aunt got her bachelor's degree in nursing and was a United States Army nurse in World War II. In the course of my growing up, I acquired a deep sense of commitment and ability to help others. My academic beginnings helped me to build skills and knowledge I needed first as a psychology major (bachelor's), then as a school teacher (Master's), and finally, as a language teacher educator (PhD). In the course of my early life, I learned to trust my inner voice – to learn from my experiences and from incredibly wonderful mentors. And I have learned to repackage my skills, knowledge, and habits as I have moved along through the past 35+ years in TESOL. Like many teachers, I have applied and taught my students some practices and habits that work for me; and in many cases, those practices have paid off for my students. But those are other stories.

English teachers working with millions of students all over the world have an extraordinary job. They work in programs in which they deserve better support for their employment and career planning efforts than they currently receive. These teachers should – but often do not – lead full and satisfying professional lives in which they provide excellence in:

- instruction,
- research and scholarly activity, and
- professional and community service – both to their institutions (employment settings) and their professional communities and associations locally, regionally, nationally, and internationally.

The goal of this book is to provide professionals in Teaching English to speakers of other languages (TESOL) at all stages of their career paths with the information they need to advocate for themselves with evidence-based information to support them throughout their careers. While generally omitted from conversations on policy and society in general, TESOLers' voices are needed to anticipate any hope for the future of all English language learners. In our field, in particular, instruction often occurs in under-resourced, poorly understood, low status, and disenfranchised programs – among teachers and learners alike. This book serves to support educators' efforts to improve their own work lives through intentional and informed CPD.

The premise is that happy, engaged, and well-prepared professional teachers will produce happy, engaged, and well-prepared students. And this means all teachers – native- and non-native English speakers, in all geographical contexts worldwide who are teaching learners of all levels of proficiency and social strata, with any first and/or other languages, in all sociolinguistic contexts.

TESOL CPD has sometimes been confused with TESOL professional development. But they differ. It is important to clarify the scope and context of this book. Here, I define TESOL CPD as follows.

TESOL CPD is a description of how individuals proceed in their professional lives. As an interdisciplinary concept, TESOL CPD draws on work in language teacher education, teacher motivation, organizational development, leadership, and life balance.

In their introduction to *International Handbook on the Continuing Professional Development of Teachers*, Day and Sachs (2004) help to show how CPD differs from professional development in international settings and begin to reveal the importance of TESOL CPD as a critical element for professional development at all stages of our careers:

> … what passes for professional development in many contexts may be naïve and uninspiring and in other contexts it is an essential intellectual and emotional endeavour that rests at the heart of dedicated efforts to improve the quality of education. In these contexts, professional development for teachers uses our best knowledge about pedagogy, about professional renewal and growth, about individual commitment and about organizational life and change. It enhances the preparation of new teachers, renews the professional skills and enthusiasm of classroom veterans, even those who may feel disenchanted or disenfranchised, and improves the professional expertise, self-confidence and commitment of all. (p. xii)

Careful study of TESOL CPD begins to help us to see that "teachers' uses of our best knowledge about pedagogy …" is too often defined by others and not by teachers themselves working, as we all do in TESOL, in highly diverse

6 Introduction

professional and employment contexts with a wide range of issues, challenges, power dynamics, and standards. It is teachers, themselves, who are the rightful subject and recipients of the professional development they experience and how they apply it. Professional development, therefore, is a part of CPD; but it is not all of it. So, while teachers are accountable to using their best knowledge about pedagogy, the profession has failed to support teachers in doing so. Here, I hope to help the profession to provide teachers with tools they need in order to assure teachers being able to do their jobs well and with a sense of satisfaction and ease throughout their careers.

Somewhat better in its efforts to support teachers, a recent white paper (from Cambridge University Press, April 2018) places emphasis on interpretations by others of teachers' needs for continuing professional development with little or no attention to those teachers' own descriptions of their own career paths:

> A contextually sensitive and responsive programme of professional development for teachers designed on the basis of these principles, resourced adequately and supported by senior management is likely to provide a viable alternative to the ineffective CPD models and practices that still abound in many institutions. (Richardson & Maggioli, 2018, p. 16)

In this book, I have attempted to address a gaping omission in TESOL scholarly literature by outlining key factors in TESOL CPD based on the stories and words of teachers themselves by drawing on some examples of teachers at various stages of their careers: preservice, novice/beginners, mid-career/career switcher, veteran, and semiretired teachers. While we know a great deal about stages of development for learners of English, teachers have been ignored. In-depth descriptions of these five stages are presented in Chapter 2.

In addressing TESOL CPD, I try hard to use teachers' own voices and to the extent possible, give readers a more accurate version of TESOL career paths of a number of teachers than one gets when career paths are defined by others or when focus is only placed on professional development experiences. No two TESOL career paths are the same. However, the examples offered here can provide readers with opportunities to begin to analyze their own career paths and share those. In the end, it is my sincere hope that teachers' own voices in TESOL CPD can be contextually relevant advocacy tools for millions of TESOL professionals worldwide at all stages of their careers.

In the opening of his 1992 book, Peter Thomson describes the career of William Shakespeare:

> Shakespeare was a supremely successful accommodator. The story of his career ... shows the accommodation of his remarkable talents to the circumstances of his time: the social, political and professional life of

Elizabethan and Jacobean England. It also describes a background of theatrical rivalry, opportunism, service to noble patrons, and the sometimes involuntary involvement in political intrigue.

As we head into the second decade of the 21st century, the career paths of English language teachers worldwide also describe the work of extraordinary accommodators – just like Shakespeare! How did Shakespeare manage to "accommodate" to the challenges he faced?

TESOL professionals today face profound threats to their careers. And the remarkable story told in the volume introduced above by Thomson about Shakespeare – known worldwide as one of the most remarkable literary geniuses of all time – and his job are striking in their common themes of worry about withdrawal of funds (and for Shakespeare, "royal patronage"), the spread of disease, anxieties of war, and uncertain climate (Thomson, 1992, unnumbered page).

In many respects, the careers of English language teachers worldwide appear to contain overall positive, cheerful, and abiding workdays with generally positive experiences. Helping people learn English – a language of communication among all who lead in today's world – should be the making of a truly satisfying professional life. In fact, an English teacher might well have "the best job on earth," as her workdays are described by one TESOL professional.

While Dornyei and Ushioda (2011) describe teachers "as a body of highly qualified professionals with an intrinsically motivated and ideologically coloured commitment to pursue what they see as a largely fulfilling job," there are numerous aspects of the job that limit or threaten teachers' job security, sense of satisfaction, and sense of being appreciated for what we do.

To be sure, other than through the kindness of a friend, family member, or colleague to offer anecdotal support and kindness, until now, there is no valid way to guide or to motivate language teachers who find themselves at a crossroads in their work lives. In addition, again other than anecdote ("This worked for me," or "Why don't you just do this?"), there is almost no research and no basis for advice for teachers seeking to move ahead in their professional lives. This gaping omission in research represents a significant threat to teachers' careers and is the foundation of the proposed volume.

How do TESOLers draw on our educational backgrounds, experiences with teaching, research, and service for satisfying careers now and in the future? And while other teachers and other professional groups struggle too, TESOLers are special for their unique education and skills. The professional career path opportunities and challenges we face are different from those of others for many reasons, not the least significant of which are the fact that geography, distances, cultural differences, and languages represent no limits,

8 Introduction

as those may be in many other professional communities. As we move along through our TESOL careers, we draw on our education and experiences – both in and outside of our professional work – and contribute those in new "packages" as we age.

Taking an interdisciplinary approach, the proposed volume offers rigorous content and engaging, readable chapters describing TESOL CPD.

In a fast-changing world where technology, the appearance of the classroom itself, and changes in curriculum and assessment are all significant factors, it is not those features that are critical to the learning that happens, but rather, the most important part of learning anything – a new language included – is the teacher (Umbach & Wawrzynski, 2005, among others). It's the role of the teacher that is changing the most.

How do teachers prepare for all of these changes? And how can TESOL professionals recapture the joy of their work while managing their careers in ways that serve their professional and personal goals? The paths of some extraordinary teachers who deal with so many changes throughout their careers form the content of this book.

Career path books addressing a dozen or more professional groups are many; but few address teachers. In a brief review of available sources, I did find books and journal articles addressing CPD for librarians, musicians, scientists, biotechnicians, health professionals of all types and levels, caregivers, managers, social workers, women in engineering, science and technology, and "high achieving" women.

There have been no books on TESOL CPD until now. It is my hope that this book will provide teachers with skills to advocate for themselves, will lead teacher education programs to provide better and more intentional instruction for advocacy and intentionality in career path planning, and, finally, a strong basis for professional associations to begin to do a better job of providing relevant and useful training modules for ongoing professional development.

What TESOL Career Path Development Is *Not?*

This is not a self-help book. The book is not intuition and it does not have all the answers. The book is also not about organizational development (focus on the organization or institution), but rather this book is focused on the individual teacher in the context of his/her professional life (with implications for English language programs and for teacher education). Finally, this book is not a tool kit. Readers will find useful information that can be used to apply to a plan of career development and/or change, but the book is not a "quick" or "easy" solution to professional development needs and challenges.

Through a series of stories and research in five related disciplines – language teacher education, teacher motivation, organizational development, leadership, and life balance – we identify initial answers to complex questions about our professional lives. Drawing on the collective experiences and some published research in CPD in other fields, this book is designed to establish TESOL CPD as a unique subspecialty and to help readers to answer some of their questions, to provide some guidance, and to allay some fears.

Methodology

As both a social and cultural construct, CPD is a mechanism for visualizing professional behavior and activities over the course of one's professional life. To understand CPD, I piloted and then conducted open-ended interviews with more than 50 teachers at all stages of their careers: preservice, novice, mid-career, end of career, and retirement. I then identified the following components of CPD: language teacher education, teacher motivation, organizational development, and life balance. From those interviews, I have determined a model, milestones, and impact of CPD.

The results indicate that CPD is an inevitable, healthy process that starts long before teachers enter classrooms and extends beyond their last job well into retirement. In short, CPD is a lifelong process for TESOLers. If we knew more about it, CPD might help individual teachers to advocate on their own behalf. In addition, language programs and professional associations might do a better job of raising the bar of excellence in English language teaching.

Structure

The book moves from this introductory background through a series of chapters identifying components of CPD and ends with a conclusion and several implications, from which readers may go forward, hopefully, to use the information to improve their own professional careers.

Here, in Chapter 1, the stage is set for the introductory presentation of a theoretical foundation, which appears in full in Chapter 2. The five chapters that follow describe each of the components of CPD (Chapter 3: language teacher education, Chapter 4: teacher motivation, Chapter 5: organizational development, Chapter 6: leadership, and Chapter 7: life balance). Chapter 8 presents milestones and impact of CPD; it addresses rewards and challenges faced by teachers throughout their careers, and the penultimate chapter, Chapter 9, provides for focus on critical institutions – workplaces and language teacher associations. And finally, Chapter 10 ends the book with a list of recommendations, topic by topic. I hope that the end is actually the beginning for all readers – wherever you are on your TESOL career path!

10 Introduction

Recommendations

As you prepare to read this book, I encourage you to be selfish: Think about yourself as a teacher of English to speakers of other languages – wherever you are on your career path, you will benefit from thinking about yourself and your students will benefit from your doing that. To what extent are you prepared as a self-advocate? What level of job satisfaction do you have now, have you had in a past job and do you hope for in a future job? Some teachers have enjoyed the opportunity to keep a little notebook or journal. Write down or make an audio recording of your thoughts, feelings, joys, and challenges as you read through each chapter. Some keep those private; others share those with a trusted friend, colleague, or family member. Use the reading of this book as a means of moving forward on your career path in TESOL or wherever else you might head. Most of all, enjoy the process of learning more about TESOL CPD!

References

Carter, G. W., Cook, K. W., & Dorsey, D. W. (2009). *Career paths: Charting courses to success for organizations and their employees.* Sussex: Wiley-Blackwell.

Day, C., & Sachs, J. (2004). *International handbook on the continuing professional development of teachers.* Berkshire, England: Open University.

Dornyei, Z., & Ushioda, E. (2011). *Teaching and researching motivation* (2nd ed.). New York: Routledge Taylor & Francis.

Fessler, R. (1985). *Career-long teacher education.* Springfield, IL: Charles C. Thomas.

Huberman, M. A. (1993). *The lives of teachers.* New York: Teachers College Press. *International House Journal of Education and Development.* Retrieved from http://ihjournal.com/teachers-professional-life-cycles

Richardson, S., & Maggioli, G. D. (2018). *Effective professional development: Principles and best practices.* Cambridge papers in ELT. Cambridge, UK: Cambridge University.

Steffy, B. E., & Wolfe, M. P. (2001). A life-cycle model for career teachers. *Kappa Delta Pi Record, 38*(1), 16–19. https://doi.org/10.1080/00228958.2001.10518508

Thomson, P. (1992). *Shakespeare's professional career.* Cambridge, England: Cambridge University. Retrieved from https://shenandoah.on.worldcat.org/oclc/24174208

Umbach, P. D., & Wawrzynski, M. R. (2005). Faculty do matter: The role of college faculty in student learning and engagement. *Research in Higher Education, 46*(2), 153–184. https://doi.org/10.1007/s11162-004-1598-1

2

THEORIZING TESOL CAREER PATH DEVELOPMENT

Story

In 1984, with a new PhD in hand and a job offer in a foreign country, I was terrified. As I boarded the plane holding the hand of my seven-year-old child, I felt like I was jumping off a cliff. How could a woman from one country with no experience living and working anywhere else go to another country and expect to be seen as legitimate? I was terrified I'd made a bad decision to go so very far away. How could I possibly take what I knew and could do and use it in a place I had never been with colleagues and students with whom I shared very little – maybe nothing? And it wasn't just about a new job – how could I live in a completely foreign environment and be successful in my new job? As important, what about the physical and emotional health of my family and me as we jumped off that cliff? I was to learn then – and carry it with me now every single day – 35 years later: My having accepted that job was to send me on what would become a series of extraordinary adventures and significant milestones throughout my career. And I'll return to this story later on with a description of several of those adventures and milestones.

Many TESOLers have had similar experiences, knowing well that their desire to help others includes travel to foreign countries and that their knowledge and skills may or may not translate easily into new environments. We seek to understand and achieve professional satisfaction and success. And while the same can be said for academic positions in domestic environments too, no theory-based research is currently available to guide us. And nothing had been available to do so – beyond the friendly anecdotes of encouraging friends and colleagues to help us when we face what are inevitable (and nowadays, more frequent and more difficult) career challenges – until now. I hope this book will be a first step in helping TESOL (Teachers of English to Speakers of Other Languages) professionals

12 Theorizing TESOL Career Path Development

worldwide to identify research questions and answer those. I hope too to help others find joy and deal with those inevitable challenges in their professional lives – wherever they are on their career paths.

In this chapter, I seek to provide a theoretical foundation for TESOL career path development. This information will be helpful to those who seek to do research and to get answers to important questions about our careers. Until now, many of us have relied on the kindness of friends who encourage us with anecdotal stories (like mine above) to support our efforts to engage in positive, successful, and satisfying careers and career development in TESOL. And the research that we have is on occupational choice, not how careers develop. Here, we look at sequences of occupational positions with the hope of providing TESOL career path development (CPD) with good descriptions of comprehensive theories rather than segmental ones.

Beginning with an overview and rationale, this chapter contains a description of the components of a theory for TESOL career path development. Those are TESOL teacher education, teacher motivation, organizational development, leadership, and life balance. I will outline and evaluate the relevant results of research and identify expectations for future development.

Overview

In a recent Google search for "career path development," I found 341,000,000 listings. And while I, of course, failed to review them all, I did look at several hundred of those. In all cases, the listings for career path development address "how to help your employees succeed" or "steps in creating a career path for your employees." The word "employee" stood out because in the TESOL world, we rarely address employment as a part of our canon. And there is no theory for studying TESOL career paths. There were very few examples of postings containing ways in which to address career path development for teachers, researchers, and service providers (like we are in TESOL). In addition, there was a decidedly western take on the topic with the following example being one of many taking the same position:

This career development process is where an individual fashions a work identity. In the United States, we are what we do; thus one's job becomes a person's identity. According to one source, Pennsylvania State Department of Education, K-12 (2018), it is imperative when educating our young people that our school systems assist and consider the significance of this responsibility for our youth and their future. The influences on and outcomes of career development combine with others as one aspect of professional socialization as part of a broader process of human development. Here, I hope to untangle some of these issues and with humility, recommend that future research address these in depth. Focusing on students' identities as workers, the Pennsylvania State Department of Education description here is an example of a means of applying principles to teachers, teacher education and teachers' identities as workers. Those who choose to be teachers have their identities inextricably tied to that professional role and status, just as students have.

It is in this quotation that we find the first of many problems with applying research already completed for students and for professionals who are not teachers to the TESOL profession and scholarly discipline. We don't all work in the United States; we identify with non-native English speakers; and we gain value and meaning from a variety of sources (not only classroom teaching).

Among the responses to questions on career path development in over 50 interviews conducted for the publication of this book, I had the opportunity to learn about TESOL CPD from colleagues, former students, and others. One glaring fact is that many TESOLers fail to acknowledge their own skills and knowledge.

In preparing her CV for a job application, one subject "forgot" to include the fact that she is bilingual. Another subject failed to include in her description of her skills the fact that early on in her career, she had taken a part-time job (to pay her tuition and fees) as a barista, and in addition to her responsibilities serving up coffee, she had been invited by her boss to keep the accounting records at the café where she worked. These are two of many examples of TESOLers who simply don't know or had forgotten what knowledge and skills they have to offer as they move forward in their careers. In both cases, adding those items had a significant positive impact on these professionals' career path development in TESOL.

It is the omission in our field of a theory of career path development, which leads to the publication of this book. This chapter, on theory, will guide researchers and teachers in the future as we attempt to build a research base on career path development in TESOL. A research-driven foundation for career path development is needed. In this chapter, I will try to lay out a theoretical framework for career path development in TESOL. I hope that this theoretical framework will provide support and perhaps begin to document the anecdotal efforts made by well-meaning TESOLers who try to help their colleagues, family members, and friends with advice on career path development.

As an interdisciplinary field of study, TESOL is generally agreed to be founded on three subspecialty areas: applied linguistics, pedagogy, and cross-cultural communication. In general, we now have an established canon and body of research. But in the past, we have relied on the work of others to forward our theories and research. As a multidisciplinary field of social sciences research, TESOL research finds its theoretical roots in physical sciences with generalized statements serving to facilitate broad conceptualizations about natural events. And over time, we have evolved into the use of a variety of theoretical models to support our research.

In his book on *Theories of Career Development* (2nd ed.), Osipow (1973) provides a starting point in creating a theory of TESOL career path development. He also provides us with a basis on which to draw in our effort to understand how TESOL careers develop in noting that theory, ideally, serves as a basis for conceptualizing events occurring in our careers. Theory begins with observations of events and becomes more complex as more events are involved. Theories turn into research whose predictive value allow appraisal of the validity of the theory. Theory is a tool for a scientist. Theories help us to understand events, so new understandings about the world come from theories. Osipow goes on to ask a series of questions that help us to see the value and content of a theory for TESOL career path development: Do data we collect support the predictions we make about careers? Do tests of predictions yield expected results? How general is the theory? And what is the range of phenomena the theory is capable of integrating/explaining? This is a particularly important question for TESOL career path development because of the extensive breadth we have in our field – we teach learners of all abilities, all ages, and with a wide range of unique characteristics both among the students we teach – learning styles and preferences, disabilities, first languages, and other factors – and in contexts that range from highly structured and professionally guided programs to those that rely on volunteers and extremely limited resources. How well does the theory explain what we're dealing with? Does it lead to new understandings? And how operational is the theory? A good theory covers the widest possible range of phenomena with minimal postulates.

Our first step is to consider the teacher and the situated contexts in which we engage in our professional activities. All of us adhere to the norms and values in which we live and work as well as those from which we have come our whole lives. Here, in Figure 2.1, I offer a relatively straightforward description of a way to analyze TESOL career path development. By understanding teachers

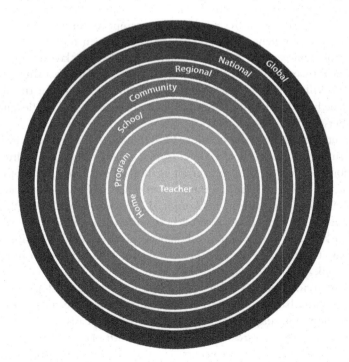

FIGURE 2.1 Context of TESOL career path development.

Theorizing TESOL Career Path Development 15

more broadly than has been the case in the past – to put teachers at the center of inquiry – we can better understand how TESOL career paths develop and evolve. How and to what extent do these contexts influence teachers at various stages of their careers: home (family members and close friends and neighbors), at work – in their program and institutional or academic institutional setting, as a part of their local communities and finally, at various levels of geographical reach – regionally, nationally and internationally.

Stages of TESOL Career Path Development

For the purposes of the analysis here, I have identified and presented in Figure 2.2 some characteristics of English as a Second Language (ESL)/ English as a Foreign Language (EFL) teachers and teacher educators – defined in the research as well as from anecdotal sources – at five career path stages for TESOLers: preservice, novice/beginner, mid-career/career switcher, veteran, and semiretired. This list is designed less to pigeonhole teachers and you'll see right away that none of these stages is a perfect description of all teachers everywhere, and interested readers and those who will pursue further study on TESOL career path

FIGURE 2.2 TESOL career path development.

16 Theorizing TESOL Career Path Development

development will want to modify these as needed for their purposes. But here, I offer a general typological continuum with the hope that it might be useful as we begin to analyze in depth TESOL career path development in today's world.

Important note/caveat: All formal teacher education is a process and all teacher education processes are situated in specific contexts of English language use and in specific social, psychological, and geographical contexts. There are hundreds of books addressing these. Here, we focus on stages of teacher development across our career paths. Readers will apply the relevant situated processes of teacher learning: teachers' classroom behaviors, teachers' pedagogy, teacher education, biological, cognitive and affective factors and connections among these processes.

Rationale for Theoretical Approach Taken Here

For some disciplines, career path development has a long history in academic research. Since the beginning of the 20th century, four dominant theories have guided that work: Holland's (1996) career typology, Super identifies self-concept as a development process informing career path development (Careers New Zealand 2012), Bandura (1989) identifies the social-cognitive aspects of career path development, and Ginsburg has been credited with the first theory of career development (Ginsberg, Ginsburg, Axelrad, & Herma, 1951). I will describe below what for some readers may be new and for others is familiar based in earlier study. For all TESOLers, this information will be new because, to my knowledge, no rationale for an approach to TESOL career path development has been published until now.

For the past 75 years or so, according to Holland and Bandura, we find interest in developing a theory for career path development. Using trait factor theory, Holland sees work satisfaction coming from a match or congruence between six dominant personality types and the type of work one does. Those are realistic, investigative, artistic, social, enterprising, and conventional. For more information on Holland's work, please consult Holland (1987). Super in Osipow (1973) presents what seems like a popular description of vocational behavior (one of the most commonly cited authors at *Science Direct* and 2,880,000 hits on Google) in two components of his theory of career development: (1) abilities to describe and evaluate self through responses to questions about self-concept and life stages as applied to work life and (2) stages of human development as applied to work: growth, exploratory, maintenance, and decline. A body of work – among four scholars and their associates – provides us with an initial foundation for research in TESOL career path development today and for the first time in this volume.

Drawing on this work and factors that may identify specific factors to TESOL, we see how and to what extent the findings described in this research apply (and don't apply) to TESOL CPD.

In this chapter, I will summarize those factors that seem to contribute to TESOL CPD as follows: TESOL teacher education, teacher motivation, organizational development, leadership, and life balance.

TESOL Teacher Education

Teacher education has a strong impact on career path development. What knowledge and skills do teachers acquire in their TESOL teacher education programs? At this time, the Master's is still considered the "terminal degree" for TESOL professionals worldwide. However, as the canon expands and the amount of knowledge and skill required for TESOL has led to the establishment of many PhDs and EdDs in our field, the Master's will still land you a good job in most institutional contexts worldwide.

Here, I will provide a summary of what knowledge and skills candidates in TESOL Master's programs acquire and must demonstrate excellence. Later, in Chapter 3, we will see ways of addressing important questions about TESOL career paths and how this extraordinary skill set might be applied throughout our careers in TESOL and in other fields as well.

In addition to the (very briefly) summarized version of the knowledge and skills required for teachers and addressed in their Master's programs, I will present an opportunity now to look more closely at four additional factors essential to our theory of TESOL CPD: teacher motivation, organizational development, leadership, and life balance.

Teacher Motivation

By nature, teachers are motivated to help others. But until the last ten years or so, the bulk of research on motivation of any kind in TESOL and applied linguistics has been focused on learner motivation and ways in which teachers must accommodate different types of learners in order to make sure they learn. Gardner and Lambert's famous 1972 research provides a typology, or classification system, for learner motivation (instrumental and integrative motivation) is well-known to all TESOLers. But rare attention was paid to the motivation that teachers bring to the classroom until relatively recently. In her chapter in Ushioda and Dörnyei's book, *Motivation, Language Identity and the L2 Self*, Kubanyiova (2009) finally begins to addresses and describes the importance of teacher motivation for the first time. She identifies a variety of factors in teacher motivation, including these important components: (1) possible selves in language teacher development, (2) links between teacher motivation and ideal self or "ought-to selves," and (3) the habit of impelling self to self-regulatory action. While using the concept of "possible self" as a lens through which to examine the motivation part of teachers' career path development in TESOL, how can we operationalize

18 Theorizing TESOL Career Path Development

and measure it? And finally, Kubanyiova addresses the critical role of context in teacher motivation.

What differences do we find in what motivates teachers at different stages of their career paths? Does a preservice teacher's motivation, for example, also motivate a teacher at another stage in his/her career? Answers to this question will help guide teachers as well as their professors and mentors toward research-based career advice and decisions rather than relying on what had previously been the efforts of kind mentors and friends with anecdotal stories that might not be as useful. We will look in more depth at teacher motivation for TESOLers in Chapter 4.

Of course, at no stage of their careers do teachers work in a vacuum, and so, it is important that we consider the role of the institutions in which teachers work every day. How and to what extent do organizations and institutions, through their structures, policies, and procedures, provide opportunities for teachers to move forward in their careers? How do organizations function in order to support teachers to navigate their career paths both within those organizations as teachers move forward there or after a teacher resigns or is terminated and moves on to another organization? In the next section, I will present how an analysis of an organization's development might provide helpful insights into ways in which teachers move along their career paths in TESOL.

Organizational Development

We all know how "the mood" or "personality" of a workplace can impact our sense of satisfaction for working there. As a graduate student at a large US-based university, I couldn't wait to get there every day. Our department and the program in which it was housed was cheerful, positive, enjoyable, and well organized. Even when challenges came, this work environment supported the professional development of all of us – students and faculty alike. Another workplace was a drag – everyone dreaded going to work; we never went early or stayed late. There were fights everywhere all the time. Organizations and how they develop and are run are key features in our career path development in TESOL. Chapter 5 will present an overview of how organizational development serves TESOLers along their career paths at all stages.

Leadership

Teachers are leaders. And in addition to their classes, teachers lead elsewhere as well. For example, many teachers choose to assume leadership roles as a part of their departmental or institutional identity with accrediting procedures; program recruitment, assessment, and development; positions in their professional associations (locally, regionally, and even nationally and internationally); and community-based service activities. In short, TESOLers are not only managers of classroom and online learning, but they also frequently stand out as leaders in a variety of tasks related to their primary role as teachers. Such leadership positions might be in terms of professional and/or community service projects, as well as in creative work and publishing. Leadership skills are essential for professional career path development in TESOL. What leadership skills influence TESOL professionals across their careers? As a novice teacher, how does one get leadership experience (when surrounded by those with more experience and larger networks)? How do we build TESOL leadership skills and to what extent do those skills help us along our career paths?

While focused squarely on US-based K-12 teaching contexts, Association for Supervision and Curriculum Development (ASCD) offers an extraordinary example of an organization that encourages and provides open access leadership training for members. In a recent article published by ASCD in a magazine called *Educational Leadership*, Harrison and Killion (2007) offer ten leadership roles for teachers. In part they write this valuable insight for TESOLers:

> Teachers exhibit leadership in multiple, sometimes overlapping, ways. Some leadership roles are formal with designated responsibilities. Other more informal roles emerge as teachers interact with their peers. The variety of roles ensures that teachers can find ways to lead that fit their talents and interests. Regardless of the roles they assume, teacher leaders shape the culture of their schools, improve student learning, and influence practice among their peers.

Along their career paths, TESOLers do the same. We find ways to lead both formally and informally. And we do that in extremely diverse contexts of work and English language teaching. In one country, where students all speak the same first language, English teachers find ways to support their students in using English through Internet-based social media exchanges with others using English, on Skype and other real-time connections that allow for authentic communication at a distance when there may be limited opportunities to do that locally. Teachers find ways of helping students develop written language using project-based assignments where they engage readers who are outside the classroom setting in order to provide authentic reader-writer interactions. Lessons are not all teacher leaders prepare off-hours (when they're not physically in the classroom). Teacher leaders work with local colleagues on preparing local or regional professional development activities. Teacher leaders identify an instructional challenge and set about to organize an action research project, then present their findings to colleagues in their own organization or beyond at a local teachers' meeting or conference. As they progress on their career paths, some teacher leaders find themselves moving ahead and working with national or even international organizations as officers or mentors, or in other professional organizational roles. Chapter 6 addresses the key role of leadership in TESOL career path development.

Life Balance

In these times of international, national, and even regional and local turmoil, it is no secret that individuals seek solace and hope in a variety of ways. Recent psychology and human resources research address self-care for reasons described in Chapter 1, TESOL professionals worldwide need balance in their lives too. Finding tools to balance our lives throughout our career paths in TESOL and the connection between life balance and career path development in TESOL is a part of what we do as professionals. According to a recent report from the Institute for Employment Studies (2007) in the United Kingdom, employers are doing more to address life balance issues as work forces become more. Demographic changes, a more diverse workforce, business imperatives, and government policy have combined to force employers to pay new attention in recent decades to life balance issues. More attention is paid now to ways in which workers are using time at work as well as time outside work to address health and well-being in their lives. And one report even identifies "High-performance management practices, working hours and work-life balance" (White, Hill, McGovern, Mills, & Smeaton, 2003).

For TESOL professionals, challenges to life balance include those above, faced by those in other professions, but challenges intensified with new challenges by the 21st-century world of international travel, nonresident employment (when traveling to work in a country different from one's own), security and safety issues of international travel and living, and the challenges faced by non-native English-speaking TESOL professionals worldwide. Chapter 7 presents a start to our understanding of how life balance may be the most significant factor of all factors in understanding TESOL career path development. We will explore this connection – between life balance and career path development in TESOL – as the final section in my analysis of a start of a theory for TESOL career path development.

A Start – Theoretical Model for TESOL Career Path Development

Here is a brief overview of the research model proposed for TESOL career path development. I have added some preliminary definitions and notes.

Factors Influencing Teacher Development and Stages of Teacher Development

A research model for TESOL career path development requires a description of how various factors influence teachers at different stages of their professional development. In order to initiate the discussion, I have conducted a literature review and drawn on it as well as personal experience (including that of former students, current and past colleagues, and others). What follows is a short summary of that effort. The remaining chapters of this book will address details for the information in summary form below.

An initial review of literature across a wide range of fields provides us with a preliminary description of factors that seem to be important over the course of their careers for many TESOL professionals. While these factors reflect what many researchers in other fields have found for their groups, here are some definitions and notes to guide further discussion and research on TESOL career path development. However, the impact of these factors will change based on the stage in which one finds himself/herself. And so, in addition to the four factors, I also present five stages of career path development. Later chapters will consider these factors and how the impact each carries on teachers at each of the five stages of professional development.

Note: Though few published research results are available for TESOL professionals, Farrell (2012) is a single notable exception. Where possible, references to research on each stage and each characteristic are provided. In other cases, the characteristic is based purely on anecdotal evidence (no reference provided).

Four essential *factors* in TESOL career path development are as follows:

Professional Identity/Motivation

Dealt with in greater detail in Chapter 4, teacher motivation is defined as follows: According to Dörnyei (2014), motivation is "responsible for *why* people decide to do something, *how long* they are willing to sustain the activity, and *how hard* they are going to pursue it" (p. 519). In addition, Ushioda (2003) describes teacher motivation in the context of a classroom where teacher motivation has been shown to interrelate with student motivation. The teacher is a class member and must find "stimulation so that learners will discover things they want to do for themselves." Here, we find an overlap between teachers and students. This is a fascinating idea and one to which we'll return. So, for our purposes, motivation is observable and we can see the extent to which a teacher is motivated.

Attitudes

While attitudes and motivation are often collapsed into a single category, I have determined the value of keeping them separate here. Here is an explanation for that decision: Too often, teacher motivation is misunderstood. Attitudes, on the other hand, are not directly observable. Rather, most attitudes research contains strict reliance on self-reported data: What is your attitude toward X? How do you feel about student behavior x, colleague y, etc.? Attitudes are not directly observable. Still, they are very important, in my view, to descriptions of teachers' career path development.

Efficacy/Skills

Efficacy here refers to the extent to which a teacher has the ability to achieve whatever result he/she anticipates. Skills are the teaching tools he/she has to enable excellence in student learning. As we move along our career paths in TESOL, we change in terms of our expertise, how we handle work-related challenges, and our sense of how well we are doing our jobs.

Career Trends

Career trends are the general directions we see our careers going. Like trends on social media where we find "popularity trends" to guide what users talk about, use their time and energy, and the way attention turns, career trends change as we proceed along our careers in TESOL. What do we do with our time? How do we progress as professionals and as individuals as we get older in TESOL?

Stages of Development

In addition to identifying factors influencing our careers, the following is a description of stages of development for many TESOL professionals from the beginning to the end of their careers.

Here are five categories of many teachers' developmental stages across their careers.

Preservice Teachers

Teachers who are working toward a degree or certificate in TESOL who aren't employed full-time in professional teaching positions.

Novice/Beginners

These are teachers in their first professional jobs (with opportunities for promotion and tenure as well as health and retirement benefits) in teaching English to speakers of other languages; in most cases, these teachers have academic credentials but have only professional experience in the context of a training program (for example, a practicum assignment as a part of their Master's degrees in TESOL). While there is general agreement that "novice" refers to a teacher's first year on the job, there is a handful of other sources that extend "novice" to as many as three years (for example, the home page of the website for a reputable organization entitled IGI Global, 2018).

In my story (above), I place myself as a "novice teacher." When I took the job described, I had considerable experience teaching English to speakers of other languages. But I was a novice/beginner as a first-time ever as a paid, full-time teacher educator, which was the position to which I was going in the story.

Novice teachers bring a variety of strengths and weaknesses to a new teaching position. Some novice teachers are not young (I will address "career switchers" below); but most have a youthful and current worldview. They are often enthusiastic and willing to take on more work than assigned. Tait (2008) found novice teachers to have great "resilience." And in his research, Jonathan Eckert (2016) goes so far as to call novice teachers "fearless." Were you "fearless" as a novice/beginning teacher?

As a group, novice teachers learn (more or less quickly) the value of collaboration among a wide range of those with whom they work – students, colleagues, administrators, a variety of staff members, among others (Day & Gu, 2010). In addition, they learn to manage stress (many teachers identify their first year as "a struggle for survival"), they must learn how to work with mentors (if they are fortunate enough to have one), and they must be able to reflect on what they have done that worked and what didn't work, then put those reflections into action for improving their abilities to teach (Farrell, 2008). In 2012, Farrell identifies a gap that causes problems for novice teachers who lose touch with their mentors and/or professors. This gap creates what Farrell describes as a "hazing experience," rather than real professional developmental experiences for novice teachers. With similar findings addressing teachers' need to feel a sense of safety on the job, Chubbock and her colleagues (2001) suggest an interactive process that includes person, school context, support context, and personal relationships.

Like doctors and lawyers, teachers "practice" our professional skills; and as novices, we come to accept that we learn as much as we teach in our first year(s) on the job. Of course, these are trends and generalized descriptions one can easily relate to (I hope!); they are not meant to describe specific individuals.

While there is a mass of research on novice teachers (and it is true that they differ dramatically from one another), our goal here is more to address ways in which teachers' careers are shaped and affected by their time as novices/beginners and less to review the literature on novice teachers. For our purposes, a brief list of characteristics for novice/beginners (and indeed for all of the five stages of teachers' careers) appear at the end of this chapter.

Mid-Career/Career Switchers

Mid-career teachers are those who occupy positions within institutions where they provide instruction and are compensated with the same opportunities as noted above for novice teachers. Some mid-career teachers are often assigned leadership positions and often carry other responsibilities beyond instruction (curriculum development, assessment, and administrative tasks). Career switchers are teachers who have had prior professional work experience in other fields (not TESOL). They bring their skills and knowledge from other professional positions to the TESOL workplace.

24 Theorizing TESOL Career Path Development

Veteran Teachers

These teachers are often "top earning" members of professional instructional staff but who also carry other responsibilities, administrative (similar to those above for mid-career teachers) and training tasks. Veteran teachers are those who have a history in the institution and perhaps even the English program in which they are working. This group is the fastest shrinking group of teachers in our field. In the past decade, increasingly large numbers of veteran teachers have either retired or left the field of TESOL. Having often reached the top of their pay grade, veteran teachers are expensive and are replaced by less expensive novice or mid-career-level teachers.

Semiretired Teachers

Having completed careers in ESL/EFL, these are teachers who maintain short-term or part-time positions. While consultancies worldwide are available for semiretired teachers, most engage in local schools, colleges, or universities where they live. Table 2.1 shows the characteristics of English language teachers at five career path stages.

In the next chapters, I explore these characteristics in depth and with an eye on ways of operationalizing these ideas while promoting the necessity of more research on TESOL career path development.

Recommendations

My own research has revealed the factors and model presented in this chapter. I claim no private ownership for those. And there may be other factors that might be addressed as a part of research in TESOL career path development. I encourage readers to review this presentation of theory and consider ways in which it may be useful to you as a researcher and as a professional in TESOL. In later chapters, I address a variety of issues that emanate from this theoretical description; and there are hopefully ideas here that readers will take away and explore in more depth on their own. Please note that each chapter contains a *References* section of this chapter (and all chapters in this book, as well as a complete listing at the end of this book), in which detailed background sources can be found, accessed, and reviewed. Those are also helpful to those who want to dive deeper into TESOL career path development theory.

In considering one's own career path, it is sometimes useful to identify (a) where we are now, and (b) among the factors identified here, which ones may be the most important to you? Right now, are there causes, conditions, and/or circumstances that may protrude in your daily life, things that might be bubbling up in your mind on a regular basis? Like me and some colleagues of my own, do you feel like your education might need a retooling? Do you feel demotivated

TABLE 2.1 Characteristics of English language teachers at five career path stages

	Identity/motivation as a teacher	*Attitudes/beliefs*	*Efficacy/skills*	*Career trends*
Preservice	Conscientious, malleable, academically oriented, varied interests, focused on student problems (Decker & Rimm-Kaufman, 2008), high commitment and lower stress (Klassen & Chiu, 2011)	Extraverted, agreeable, cooperative	Self-conscious, tense	Commitment determines decision to stay/leave the teaching profession (Klassen & Chiu, 2011)
Novice/ beginner	Enthusiastic, willing to take on too large work assignments, follow (but need) guides for reflection (Pultorak, 1996)	Youthful, current world view, fearless (Eckert, 2016), reliant (West, Dyrbye, Erwin, & Shanafelt, 2016)	Limited skills in collaboration, stressed (a hazing experience; Farrell, 2012), need sense of safety (Chubbuck, Clift, Allard, & Quinlan, 2001)	Increased use of professional literature and scholarly research, yet mixed use of professional development opportunities (Richter, Kunter, Klusmann, Ludtke, & Baumert, 2011)
Mid-career and career switcher	Motivated for professional enhancement (Richter et al, 2011), career adaptable (Brown, Bimrose, Barnes, & Hughes, 2012), understands value of research development (Griffiths, Thompson, & Hryniewicz, 2014)	Self-identify as experienced and confident (Celep, 2000)	Reliance on past work experiences (sometimes in TESOL, sometimes elsewhere)	Career change more common among males than females (Johnson & Birkeland, 2003)

(Continued)

TABLE 2.1 Characteristics of English language teachers at five career path stages (*Continued*)

	Identity/motivation as a teacher	Attitudes/beliefs	Efficacy/skills	Career trends
Veteran	Organized and attendance to detail and tenacity and commitment (Megyeri, 1996, as reported in Edwards, 2003)	Personal concerns more important than work, and material over intrinsic benefits	Institutional and/or ESL program experience; rely on procedural knowledge (Watt, Richardson, & Smith, 2017), strong scheduling abilities, ability to handle discipline problems	"Top earners" and fastest shrinking group in many programs perception of limited career possibilities
Semiretired	Usually adjunct and/or often short-term consultants, resilience and loss of work identity, emotional labor and commitment (Kirk & Wall, 2010), identity continuity and leisure focus (Atchley, 1971)	Relaxed, works for pleasure of contacts with students and colleagues. Not as concerned about material benefits (personal communication, 2018)	Mature values and wisdom	Women's retirement as continuity and change experience choice and constraints (Duberle, Carmichael, & Smzigin, 2013).

lately? What aspects of the organization where you work seem to be in the lime-light lately? Are there colleagues who've been particularly supportive (or not)? Are there new challenges for you at work? What experiences do you have with leadership and what impact have those had on others? Are those items that might be added to your CV now? And finally, how is your life balance? Are you feeling like you've got a sense of balance in your life? What is there too much of? What do you need more? It may or may not be possible to do anything about these or other issues; but the simple act of attending to those, writing them down now – these are all potentially helpful steps for your career path development.

In addition to research about one's own career path, there is potential for better understandings about the factors that influence teachers in each phase. For example, a preservice teacher's motivation is likely different from that of a veteran teacher. Defining and then measuring these factors fully demand careful research design. I hope this volume will get that ball rolling. For now, we will move to descriptions of the factors contributing to TESOL career path develop-ment, starting with the big one, teacher education.

References

Atchley, R. C. (1971). Retirement and leisure participation: Continuity or crisis? *The Gerontologist, 11*(1), 13–17. https://doi.org/10.1093/geront/11.1_Part_1.13

Bandura, A. (1989). Human agency in social cognitive theory. *American Psychologist, 44* (9), 1175–1184. Retrieved from http://www.stiftelsen-hvasser.no/documents/Bandura_Human_Agency_in_social_Cognitiv_theory.pdf

Brown, A., Bimrose, J., Barnes, S-A., & Hughes, D. (2012). The role of career adaptabili-ties for mid-career changers. *Journal of Vocational Behavior, 80*, 754–761. https://doi.org/10.1016/j.jvb.2012.01.003

Careers New Zealand. (2012). Donald Super developmental self-concept [PDF file]. Retrieved from https://www.careers.govt.nz/assets/pages/docs/career-theory-model-super.pdf

Celep, C. (2000). The correlation of the factors: The prospective teacher's sense of effi-cacy and beliefs, and attitudes about student control [Abstract]. *National Forum of Teacher Educational Administration and Supervision Journal, 17E*(4). Retrieved from https://eric.ed.gov/?id=ED451157

Chubbuck, S. M., Clift, R. T., Allard, J., & Quinlan, J. (2001). Playing it safe as a novice teacher: Implications for programs for new teachers. *Journal of Teacher Education, 52*(5), 365–376.

Day, C., & Gu, Q. (2010). *The new lives of teachers*. London, UK: Routledge. https://doi.org/10.4324/9780203847909

Decker, L., & Rimm-Kaufman, S. (2008). Personality characteristics and teacher beliefs among pre-service teachers. *Teacher Education Quarterly, 35*(2), 45–64. Retrieved from http://www.jstor.org/stable/23479223

Dörnyei, Z. (2014). Motivation in second language learning. In M. Celce-Murcia., D. Brinton, M. A. Snow, & D. Bohlke (Eds.), *Teaching English as a second or foreign language* (4th ed.). Boston, MA: Cengage Learning.

28 Theorizing TESOL Career Path Development

Duberle, J., Carmichael, F., & Smzigin, I. (2013). Exploring women's retirement: Continuity, context and career transition. *Gender, Work and Organization, 21*(1), 71–90. https://doi.org/10.1111/gwao.12013

Eckert, J. (2016). *The novice advantage: Fearless practice for every teacher*. Thousand Oaks, CA: Corwin – A Sage Publication.

Edwards, E. A. (2003). *Retention and motivation of veteran teachers* (Electronic theses and dissertations, paper 742). Retrieved from http://dc.etsu.edu/etd/742

Farrell, T. S. C. (2008). Here's the book, go teach the class: ELT practicum support. *RELC Journal, 39*(2), 226–241. https://doi.org/10.1177/0033688208092186

Farrell, T. S. C. (2012). Novice-service language teacher development: Bridging the gap between preservice and in-service education and development. *TESOL Quarterly, 46*(3), 435–449. https://doi.org/10.1002/tesq.36

Gardner, R. C., & Lambert, W. E. (1972). *Attitudes and motivation in second language learning*. Rowley, MA: Newbury House Publishers.

Ginsberg, E., Ginsburg, S. W., Axelrad, S., & Herma, J. L. (1951). *Occupational choice: An approach to a general theory*. New York, NY: Columbia University Press.

Griffiths, V., Thompson, S., & Hryniewicz, L. (2014). Landmarks in the professional and academic development of mid-career teacher educators. *European Journal of Teacher Education, 37*(1), 74–90. http://dx.doi.org/10.1080/02619768.2013.825241

Harrison, C. H., & Killion, J. (2007). Ten roles for teacher leaders. *Educational Leadership, 65*(1). Retrieved from http://www.ascd.org/publications/educational-leadership/sept07/vol65/num01/Ten-Roles-for-Teacher-Leaders.aspx

Holland, J. L. (1987). Current status of Holland's theory of careers: Another perspective. *Career Development Quarterly, 36*(1), 24–30.

Holland, J. L. (1996). Exploring careers with a typology: What we have learned and some new directions. *American Psychologist, 51*(4), 397–406. http://dx.doi.org/10.1037/0003-066X.51.4.397

Institute for Employment Studies. (2007, March). *Annual review* (PDF file). Retrieved from https://www.employment-studies.co.uk/system/files/resources/files/annrev07.pdf

International Publisher of Information Science and Technology Research (2018). *IGI Global*. Retrieved from https://www.igi-global.com/

Johnson, S. M., & Birkeland, S. E. (2003). Pursuing a "sense of success": New teachers explain their career decisions. *American Educational Research Journal, 40*(3), 581–617. https://doi.org/10.3102/00028312040003581

Kirk, J., & Wall, C. (2010). Resilience and loss in work identities: A narrative analysis of some retired teachers' work-life histories. *British Educational Research Journal, 36*(4), 627–641. Retrieved from https://www.jstor.org/stable/27823636

Klassen, R. M., & Chiu, M. M. (2011). The occupational commitment and intention to quit of practicing and pre-service teachers: Influence of self-efficacy, job stress, and teaching context. *Contemporary Educational Psychology, 36*(2), 114–129. Retrieved from https://ac.els-cdn.com/S0361476X11000038/1-s2.0-S0361476X11000038-main.pdf?_tid=230b042a-baaf-4dc8-8a8a-378eadbcf144&acdnat=1544717694_b231a3ec4bd965ba09aba7d0793b5a27

Kubanyiova, M. (2009). Possible selves in language teacher development. In E. Ushioda & Z. Dörnyei (Eds.), *Motivation, language identity and the L2 self* (pp. 314–332). Bristol, UK: Multilingual Matters.

Megyeri, K. A. (1996). Tribute. *English Journal, 85*, 24–29.

Osipow, S. H. (1973). *Theories of career development.* New York, NY: Appleton-Century-Crofts.

Pennsylvania State Department of Education, K-12. (2018). Career Ready PA. Retrieved from https://www.education.pa.gov/K-12/CareerReadyPA/Pages/default.aspx

Pultorak, E. G. (1996). Following the developmental process of reflection in novice teachers: Three years of investigation. *Journal of Teacher Education, 47*(4), 283–291. https://doi.org/10.1177/0022487196474006

Richter, D., Kunter, M., Klusmann, U., Ludtke, O., & Baumert, J. (2011). Professional development across the teaching career: Teachers' uptake of formal and informal learning opportunities. *Teaching and Teacher Education, 27*(1), 116–126. https://doi.org/10.1002/tesq.36

Tait, M. (2008). Resilience as a contributor to novice teacher success, commitment, and retention. *Teacher Education Quarterly, 35*(4), 57–75.

Ushioda, E. (2003). Motivation as a socially mediated process. In D. Little, J. Ridley, & E. Ushioda (Eds.), *Learner autonomy in the foreign language classroom: Teacher, learner, curriculum and assessment* (pp. 90–102). Dublin, Ireland: Authentik Language Learning Resources Ltd. Retrieved from https://www.researchgate.net/profile/David_Little2/publication/317264706_Learner_autonomy_in_the_foreign_language_classroom_teacher_learner_curriculum_and_assssment/links/592ed1eea6fdcc89e76992c0/Learner-autonomy-in-the-foreign-language-classroom-teacher-learner-curriculum-and-assssment.pdf#page=98

Ushioda, E., & Dörnyei, Z. (2009). *Motivation, language identity and the L2 self.* Bristol, UK: Multilingual Matters. Retrieved from http://search.ebscohost.com/login.aspx?direct=true&db=nlebk&AN=245456&site=bsi-liv

Watt, H. M. G., Richardson, P. W., & Smith, K. (Eds.). (2017). *Global perspectives on teacher motivation.* Cambridge, England: Cambridge University Press.

West, C. P., Dyrbye, L. N., Erwin, P. J., & Shanafelt, T. D. (2016). Interventions to prevent and reduce physician burnout: A systematic review and meta-analysis. *The Lancet, 388*(10057), 2272–2281.

White, M., Hill, S., McGovern, P., Mills, C., & Smeaton, D. (2003). High performance management practices, working hours and work-life balance. *BJIR: An International Journal of Employment Relations, 41*(2), 75–195. https://doi.org/10.1111/1467-8543.00268

3

TEACHER EDUCATION

Overview

Formal language teacher education is essential for successful careers for teachers of English to speakers of other languages. In this chapter, we will explore how TESOL education informs and guides us in classroom teaching and research at various stages of our career paths as well as other issues for TESOL professionals as they prepare themselves for careers that take them around the world and where new tools become available every day. Staying in the TESOL profession and "ahead of the curve" is an essential task for all of us at every stage of our careers.

While academic programs of study in TESOL have in the past varied relatively little in their content, of late, many programs are carving "niche markets" where they serve the needs of teachers who seek academic study in many subspecialties. Among these subspecialty areas are English for young learners (EYL), English for some or another Specific Purpose (ESP), focus on US-based public schooling (US K-12), working with speakers of indigenous languages, and so on. In addition, there are a number of highly competitive programs leading to a certificate in TESOL, a credential that may open doors for those who may not wish to invest in an academic program. Names of certificates vary as much as quality of instruction; but there are tens of programs designed for certificate seekers and the online platform for certificates in TESOL is very popular and can be found on a number of Internet sites. One example is "The Top 15 TEFL Certificate Programs," available at https://www.bestcollegereviews.org/top/online-tefl-certificate-programs/ (Best College Reviews, n.d.).

In this chapter, we will focus on academic programs in TESOL because those are considered the standard for our profession. While certificates in TESOL may come and go and may be less valuable than academic programs in their role for TESOL career path development (CPD), academic programs of study at the postgraduate level (the Master's is considered the "terminal degree" for English language teachers worldwide) are the standard bearer. And while some TESOL professionals might find a certificate to be a milestone in their professional career paths – helping them to decide to go onward in their education – I strongly encourage readers to focus on fully accredited graduate-level academic programs in TESOL in their career paths.

Most TESOL graduate-level academic programs of study nowadays have accredited online course options, drawing on markets worldwide and far away from the geographical region in which they are physically located. See England (2012) for a collection of interesting descriptions of some of the issues facing students, instructional staff, and administration of online TESOL teacher education programs in the 21st century.

While the Master's continues to be "the terminal degree" for employment in most academic and professional English language programs worldwide. A terminal degree is defined thus, a terminal degree is a university degree that can signify one of two outcomes. In some cases, it is the highest degree that can be awarded in a specific academic or professional track. In other cases, it is a degree that is awarded when a candidate completes a certain amount of coursework but does not go on to doctoral work. Some students enroll in a terminal Master's program with the goal of preparing to enter a PhD program. For certain professions and research grants it means the lowest degree to be considered qualified.

In TESOL, the Master's is the lowest degree to be considered qualified. A doctorate (PhD or EdD), however, is increasingly becoming a valuable and sometimes essential tool for a teacher seeking exciting and challenging professional positions in TESOL. In addition to specific subspecialties and courses and the increasing effort for programs to create niches in the market for education in TESOL, most all programs include standard information in these three broad areas: applied linguistics, language pedagogy, and cross-cultural communication.

Story

In 1976, I enrolled as a part-time student in a Master's in TESOL program at a large university in Wisconsin in the United States, while simultaneously teaching English as a Second Language (ESL) part-time at a local community college and working as a clerical assistant (also part-time) as at the university. I'd recently completed a Master's in elementary education in another state the year before and try as I may, was unable to get a job in any Wisconsin public school. Though I managed to get interviews and was willing to drive a long way, interviews led

32 Teacher Education

to "No thanks" messages. I had a permanent teaching license from the State of New York, Nursery through Grade 8, and was told that "out of state credentials" can make finding a job teaching in a public school difficult.

When I became pregnant the next year, the grueling schedule I was managing became untenable and something had to go: it was the Master's in TESOL program, with which I had struggled hard from the first day I enrolled. It was somewhat of a relief to have a reason (an excuse?) to let go of the torture that program brought to me each day. Since "we needed the money" from my two part-time jobs, I quit the Master's program and continued with those activities that had a pay check attached to them. And although I abandoned it (see reasons below), my enrollment in that academic program is important to the introduction of the content of this chapter on TESOL teacher education. For that reason, I will describe my experience while a part of it:

> Starting with a course (the advisor who reluctantly guided me and recommended I take) entitled "Descriptive Linguistics" (final grade of C), was followed by a language teaching methodology and materials course (final grade also C – the instructor told me I wasn't cut out to teach English to speakers of other languages). And finally, I completed a course in dialects for which I was awarded a B. The program was a painful introduction to the academic teacher education for our field at that time; and it's a bit of a miracle that I completed three courses in it.

While enrolled in a graduate program with those three courses (at a reputable university), I was teaching ESL classes to real, live humans at the community college. Perhaps the best way to describe the torture of those TESOL courses, consider the first days living in a foreign country where you have knowledge of the language used by the people there. I felt more at home on my first days in Cairo where I spoke not one word of Arabic than I did in the biweekly classes for those three courses. I had no idea how people thought this information had anything to do with what was required of teachers to do in actual classrooms with real human students. The linguistics course was, to me, like a dreadful math course in high school – rule-driven, very much a "private club" (some of the students in the class were theoretical linguistics PhD candidates and were both verbally and socially negative toward me and others enrolled in the course who were "just language teachers"). I walked in on the first day so excited to be taking a course I knew would be useful to me as a teacher: Methods? Yay! What methods and techniques might I learn to use in my classes? Materials! Hooray! I would learn more about what to look for in excellent teaching materials and maybe, just maybe how to write my own! No way. What we learned was how various dominating theories of language are reflected in how people teach (well, taught – everything in that course was addressed in the past tense since there was nothing whatsoever that addressed the present and certainly not the future either). The dialects course was interesting – it was fun to learn about my own language and how it has changed across history and geographically too. The course focused on how languages change (mostly phonetically) across rivers and mountain ranges in the United States. When a fellow graduate student from another country politely asked how this all related to dialects anywhere else, for example, in another country (like, for example, the one in which he was born), the teacher was irked, "It's the principles we teach here. You can apply those to anywhere else in the world once you've mastered them." Oh, OK. I was intimidated; and I failed to ask the obvious burning question: "So, what the hell does any of this have to do with those 25 students I'm going to meet in two hours to teach them English?" We weren't to learn about nor address how any of this actually plays out in a classroom – anywhere.

Though no one ever asked, all of these courses were, to me, generally wholly unrelated to my needs, as I understood them, to be an effective language teacher working with students I taught at the community college. And so, in spite of the fact that I had endured considerable struggle in the earlier program, it was several years later when I decided to enroll in a doctoral program. Having taught for several years in the interim, meeting others who'd completed and loved their doctoral programs, it became clear to me that there were other places to earn a graduate degree in TESOL. And in the words of Cathy Day, a colleague both in graduate school and later in Michigan, "It's a union card." I needed a union card because I wanted to be able to help others and do it with confidence. And like most of us, I also needed a paycheck.

The happy ending (everyone loves happy endings) was that my beloved University of Illinois Champaign-Urbana (UIUC) gratefully accepted me for admission into a PhD program in a newly established multidisciplinary program there entitled Second Language Acquisition and Teacher Education (SLATE). In addition to admitting me, UIUC also accepted transfer of those nine credits earned earlier. And so, I was thus released from the requirements these courses fulfilled and for which the content matched. Whew.

UIUC taught me so much. With exceptionally diverse and highly committed faculty and staff professionals across several disciplines (linguistics, education, psychology, and ESL, among others) and with friends and colleagues in classes where we loved to arrive early and stay late and in which we learned so much together (from our professors and from one another) – our lives were changed for the better. And it wasn't just the coursework that made our time there so meaningful. We learned to be colleagues, we learned the true power of teamwork, we learned to give and receive peer feedback, we learned to lead and succeed (and yes, sometimes, fail) together. You know who you are, you fabulous Illini. Thanks for the memories. And all who are reading should know that colleagues found in an excellent TESOL graduate school program like the one I completed

34 Teacher Education

at UIUC will be with you for your whole life. They will teach you as much as the professors.

So, what do we learn in graduate programs that is essential to our CPD in TESOL? We are educated and socialized for our career paths. While some of us have already taught when we enter a program of study, for others, a graduate program in TESOL (either Master's or Doctoral level) is their introduction to the field. Whether a newcomer or an experienced teacher, here's a brief description of academic teacher education. First of all, we learn academic content.

Applied Linguistics

Applications from the field of linguistics guide teacher education in TESOL. Throughout our careers, we rely on applied linguistics knowledge in order to address classroom and online teaching of English to speakers of other languages. While there are many papers in which one can find useful definitions for applied linguistics, I will use that of Sridhar (1993) since it seems to embrace both the breadth and depth of the concept as we will need it in our TESOL CPD analysis. Sridhar writes of the variety of goals and priorities that might affect the definition we choose. I will present the definition of applied linguistics followed by observations by many (though Sridhar brings forward many of the issues relevant to us in CPD) and complete this section by illustrating how applied linguistics is important to CPD in TESOL.

For purposes of our discussion, here is the definition of applied linguistics as it appears in Wikipedia. I use this one because this definition (unlike the many academic ones) reflects what TESOLers and most lay people know about and understand applied linguistics to be: "Applied linguistics is an interdisciplinary field of linguistics which identifies, investigates, and offers solutions to language-related real-life problems" (Wikipedia, August 29, 2019).

How does applied linguistics fit into our theory of TESOL CPD?

In his 1993 paper, entitled "What are applied linguistics?" Sridhar provides us with a valuable critical analysis of the role of applied linguistics in TESOL and a good reason for considering applied linguistics as a part of our CPD.

Where would an English teacher be – throughout his/her career – without applied linguistics? The fact that applied linguistics is sometimes considered to be exactly the same as language teaching (Sridhar's "narrow view"), we know well that situated time place, social factors, and culture interacting with language are key to effective teacher education. Sridhar goes on to remind us of the importance of what have elsewhere been called "hyphenated linguistics" – first and second language acquisition, pragmatics and discourse analysis, bilingualism, historical linguistics, dialectology, and others.

I first learned about "hyphenated linguistics" when studying an example in 1981, an introductory psycholinguistics course. I thought that my teacher,

Professor Howard Maclay, had invented the term. But when we (a group of always eager graduate students) asked, he explained that the term had come to him from M. A. K. Halliday. "Hyphenated linguistics" is the combination of two academic fields of study and research – one of which is linguistics and the other, well, something else. From these hyphenations, we get sociolinguistics, psycholinguistics, neurolinguistics, computational linguistics, and others. Add to these language planning, English for specific purposes, speech pathology, reading, contrastive rhetoric, and other "very, very applied" uses of linguistics (described in detail in reports from the *Annual Review of Applied Linguistics*).

While traditionalists and hardliners have at least in the recent past seen limitations and/or exclusions of teacher education as essential for whatever reasons (self-preservation, perhaps?). They have seemed to want to exclude function, performance, and context, most are described here by Sridhar, "Applied linguists feel that linguistics has historically been defined too narrowly" (p. 9). And, I would add that language teachers feel that applied linguistics has been defined too narrowly for too long. Happily, this tradition appears to have been changing in recent decades.

Teachers must have knowledge about the nature of language, second language acquisition, and language as it is used in real-world settings. Teachers must also be able to apply that knowledge to real-world learners. Like a doctor addressing patients' health issues, a teacher draws on his/her knowledge and skills to address each new class and each new student.

In the early days of her first year of her ESL teaching career at a university in Georgia (United States), a colleague had the opportunity to work in a highly competitive academic program. Students – mostly Iranians and Colombians in those days – were required to take ESL classes in order to be considered "prepared" to enter academic programs of study in engineering and sciences mostly at the graduate level. Assigned to teach pronunciation in one low proficiency level class, the teacher made the (bad) decision to force students to learn the International Phonetic Alphabet (IPA). And while these students were highly motivated, genuinely committed to succeeding in ESL, there was a massive walkout when the teacher gave them their first test on IPA and none of the students had prepared. She had a solid foundation of knowledge but failed to consider the obvious pain one must endure to learn to use a complex tool that has absolutely no significant impact on students' learning to pronounce sounds and words (and yes, a few but very few phrases) in English so others can understand what one says. It was there that my colleague learned that linguistics knowledge is useful; but it's also not the knowledge that all learners of English need. Many don't really need IPA (as committed as I was to learning it and to making sure all my engineering and science students did too). Watching this whole event unfold, I learned – here, the hard way through student revolt! – that the teacher's knowledge is not best used when directly applied to students nor forced on them to learn (unless, of course, they are linguists or English language teachers!). It was a tough and memorable

36 Teacher Education

day for us all – teachers and our students and university Intensive English Program administration too. I am certain that, now in their old age, those students still remember that teacher who forced them to learn IPA. In some part for this experience, I took a course in second language acquisition immediately after this memorable event and deep learning from a colleague on my TESOL career path.

In addition to knowing about language and language acquisition, teachers in Master's programs in TESOL also learn about teaching. Next item on our list of items that are part of TESOL teacher education and critical to our career paths is language pedagogy.

Language Pedagogy

As we learn to use concepts and principles in applied linguistics to know more about language and language learning, we must also know how learning occurs among those at all levels of language proficiency (beginners, intermediate, and advanced students) as well as age level and contexts of English language use. Language pedagogy is the means by which teachers teach and learners acquire new knowledge and skills in a given language. Pedagogy includes approach, method, and technique (Anthony, 1963). Richards and Rodgers revised these terms in 1982 with approach, design, and procedure. But the short version, relevant here to our theory of TESOL CPD is this: teachers must be prepared to address all levels of language instruction – from the mission statement described by the institution to the program-level analysis of how the courses fit together (by level of proficiency as well as across skill and course level goals) as well as details of a minute-to-minute lesson plan. In addition to the actual observable teaching, teachers also need knowledge and skills for assessing learning.

In summary, teachers must be prepared to lead and guide instruction in ways that suit the styles, communicative needs, and the context of English language use in which their students communicate with others – presently or will in the future. A tall order, you say, for a teacher education course of study. Indeed! Many teacher education programs address these and stop there.

But TESOL teacher education includes more due to the uniqueness of our field. As we will see later, it is the combination of these factors that allow TESOL careers to move in often unpredictable and always fascinating directions. Our final skill set is described here as "cross-cultural communication."

Cross-Cultural Communication

Language differences and ways in which those differences are carried by cultural differences are deeply rooted in the TESOL field. Throughout our careers, we work with non-native English speakers in contexts worldwide where we must address professional and personal issues that affect us and our students. For that reason, Master's programs in TESOL require students to understand deep issues of cross-cultural communication. Whether inside or outside the classroom, TESOL professionals deal with cross-cultural communication throughout their careers.

Among others, the work of Edward T. Hall has established the following definition of cross-cultural communication, essential to TESOL professional development with subtopics for which are as important now as they were when he wrote them down:

> It is increasingly apparent that clashes between cultural systems are not restricted to international relations. Such clashes are assuming significant proportions within our own country and are exacerbated by the overcrowding in cities. Contrary to popular belief, the many diverse groups that make up our country have proved to be surprising persistent in maintaining their separate identities. Superficially, these groups may all look alike and sound somewhat alike, but beneath the surface are manifold unstated, unformulated differences in their structuring of time, space, materials and relationships. It is these differences that often result in the distortion of meaning, regardless of intention, when people of different cultures interact (Hall, 1959, p. x).

In some respects, cross-cultural communication must be the most important part of TESOL professionals' skills and knowledge. We use our knowledge of cross-cultural communication to work with our students every day: If we teach in a native English-speaking context, we use our knowledge and skills to bond with and create rapport with our students. We know about our own cultures and we know less but express eagerness to understand the cultural backgrounds and world views of our students. We use cross-cultural communication knowledge and skills to get along. In addition, we teach cross-cultural communication skills to our students. We want them to be able to use English in order to address and engage with their own academic and professional lives and sometimes even to function in bilingual and/or bicultural personal lives.

I drew on the extraordinary work of Gerte Hofstede (2018) in one overseas assignment in Indonesia. I had lived in one dominantly Muslim country for six years before my Indonesia posting and, as did my colleagues, thought that I knew a lot about being a non-Muslim woman professional in a Muslim country. Indeed, I had even published two books on teaching Arabic as an additional language. One particular difference was that the role of students as "helpers." My previous teaching experience, at an elite university in the Middle East left me with the impression that students were unavailable as helpers (unless paid as graduate assistants). But in Indonesia, I was sent to my students by the

38 Teacher Education

department head when I had problems or questions with housing and house maintenance tasks, transportation, shopping for food, and even personal items such as towels and sheets – it was going to be the students who would come to my home and help me to procure these items and services. I was uncomfortable being told by my university department head that "Dr. Liz, you should ask your students to help you. They are supposed to do it." For me, this way of doing things seemed wrong: how could I grade a student fairly who'd come to my home in the morning, carried all of my books, laptop, data show, and handouts to class an hour before it started? My reading of Hofstede helped me to understand the differences between the United States and Indonesia on these particular dimensions: power distance (the openness of difference between rich and poor, powerful and powerless – it was new to me), and individualism (the ways in which groups function in an academic environment). And at the same time, these were concepts I taught my students. So, in addition to helping me manage cross-cultural communications on sensitive and difficult issues (such as having a student wait on me hand and foot), I was teaching these concepts to my students, who received them with great enthusiasm. Linguistic knowledge – drawing on my earlier example of teaching IPA to my students in Georgia earlier in my career – seems less easily transmitted on the two levels identified here: (1) using the concepts in one's own daily life and (2) teaching students those same concepts as a matter of course content. Cross-cultural communication is an essential part of CPD.

Summary and Next Steps

English teachers worldwide draw on and use their knowledge and skills in applied linguistics, pedagogy, and cross-cultural communication in order to manage their professional identities as well as their day-to-day work tasks. In Chapter 10, we will look more closely at these and other questions on TESOL CPD. How do teachers use these in their careers? How and to what extent does a preservice teacher differ from a veteran teacher drawing on and applying her knowledge and skills in these areas? And as important, how does a teacher apply and adapt his/her knowledge and skills in TESOL with different knowledge and skills (outside of TESOL) acquired elsewhere? These are initial steps, the beginning of a list of interesting and until now unanswered questions for TESOL CPD.

In recent years, a number of professional associations have begun to address members' needs for opportunities to address CPD. One example, TESOL International Association, has established Professional Learning Networks (PLNs) to address teachers' ongoing professional development needs throughout their careers. Serving both those who want to address concerns related to employment and careers within the TESOL profession as well as those in transition from careers outside TESOL into positions in our profession (career switchers and other newcomers to our profession), PLNs are great tools for connecting with colleagues, finding resources for use in teaching and research, and yes, even new job prospects as one moves along in his/her career path. And those who have identified careers in to which they plan to plant themselves for the long term, personal learning environments can be valuable resources for developing skills and knowledge on one's own.

In addition to the academic content of a graduate program, TESOL professionals who seek graduate programs of study must learn other skills as well. And while some programs already address some of these, many would benefit from revisiting requirements in line with more attention than paid in the past to CPD for their current students and alumni: Those skills include socialization into a professional identity, ethics and values of professional interaction, advocacy for teachers and programs, the importance and power of engaging in a research agenda throughout one's career and the value of community service at the local, regional, national, and international levels.

How and to what extent does formal academic study in TESOL influence our career paths?

Bluntly stated, it is my claim that formal academic study has a highly significant impact on our career paths. Research is needed to help us know more about how and to what extent this claim is true. And the final chapter of this book contains some research questions for your consideration.

If I had ended my studies at the first university described above in my story (the unhappy story), it's unlikely I'd ever have become an ESL teacher educator. In fact, all of us who have known excellent graduate education in TESOL possess a skills set and a knowledge base that is at the core of our identities. Had I not left that first program and found the one at the UIUC, I would certainly not have been a TESOLer for the past three decades; and it's almost certain that I'd never be writing this book.

I would never have met some of the extraordinarily gifted professors at UIUC; and certainly, I would never have met and worked on so many wonderful and satisfying professional courses and projects in my career in TESOL. The friends, students, and colleagues I have made along the way would likely have been replaced with some nice people. But quite honestly, I would not trade the TESOLers I know now (some for many years) for anyone on this planet.

This section is incomplete without reference to the opposite story: Not all of us have had such a great time in our academic graduate programs. Some TESOLers have known extreme pain and suffering at the hand of programs poorly matched to their skills and interests; others have had difficulties fulfilling requirements; there are stories fit for novels (some have been written!) about the trials of academic life for graduate students; TESOL is no exception. And like my story, others' stories with less happy endings are important too. Those stories need to be told. Our career paths – whether happy- or sad-ending

40 Teacher Education

ones – are worth telling. We need to know how career paths go along and how graduate study affects their direction and pace. To what extent did your own graduate study influence your career path? The answers to this question will help future TESOLers to learn from our career paths.

My goal here is to describe the components of TESOL teacher education and to show how those have an impact on our career paths. In addition, I hope to have identified some critical additions for those prospective candidates and students seeking to select a graduate program in TESOL, and for those academic colleagues who seek to improve current programs and for those who hope to start new ones.

Recommendations

Teacher education programs for TESOLers is a well-established sub-specialty with a research canon and a large international community of practice. Hundreds of programs worldwide offer strong foundational knowledge and opportunities for skills development. Teachers are prepared in these programs to address the instructional learning and communication needs of learners of all ages and all levels of proficiency. In addition, in-service professional development focusing on traditional learner and learning issues is not enough.

The traditional and narrow focus on content – applied linguistics, pedagogy, and cross-cultural communication along with various specialty areas – is not enough for the TESOL professional's career in the 21st century. Teachers nowadays need skills in addressing employment and job preparation and how to navigate CPD – how to advocate for and attain recognition, opportunities for advancement, and awards for teaching, research, and service. They need to address image: the general impression that a teacher makes in a job interview, a presentation, or leading a meeting. What are the "optics" you project on camera? In the classroom, when you are in a meeting on your research, or in a conflict situation? Do you know how to leave a toxic job? TESOLers need better and more intentional instruction in online teaching in addition to traditional face-to-face instructional models. They need to be prepared to do, not only to consume, classroom-based research; and they must be prepared to engage in community and professional service activities.

Many TESOL graduate programs are beginning to address these career path issues and others too. But there's work to do in TESOL teacher education that intentionally and adequately addresses teachers' needs. Changes will lead to infusing job preparation better into the curriculum, more teacher-created research that is relevant to the legitimate and identified needs of local, regional, national, and international issues, more relevant and valued professional service projects. With these changes, teachers will be better prepared for all stages of their career paths, including the overall and much needed change in teacher image.

Finally, teachers themselves need to select educational training programs that meet their needs, address CPD, and will serve them throughout their careers. More on this subject is in Chapter 10, "It's On Us: Intentional Career Path Development."

References

Anthony, E. M. (1963). Approach, method, and technique. *ELT Journal, 17*(2), 63–67. https://doi.org/10.1093/elt/XVII.2.63.

Best College Reviews. (n.d.). The top 15 TEFL certificate programs. Retrieved from https://www.bestcollegereviews.org/top/online-tefl-certificate-programs/

England, L. (2012). *Online language teacher education: TESOL perspectives.* NY: Routledge Taylor-Francis Publishers.

Hall, E. T. (1959). *The silent language.* NY: Random House – Anchor Books.

Hofstede, G. J. (2018). Cultural comparison – Indonesia and the United States. Retrieved from https://www.hofstede-insights.com/country-comparison/indonesia,the-usa/

Richards, J. C., & Rodgers, T. (1982), Method: Approach, design, and procedure. *TESOL Quarterly, 16*, 153–168. https://doi.org/10.2307/3586789

Sridhar, S. (1993). What is applied linguistics? *International Journal of Applied Linguistics, 3*(1), 3–16. https://doi.org/10.1111/j.1473-4192.1993.tb00040.x

Wikipedia. (2019, August 29). Applied Linguistics. Retrieved https://en.wikipedia.org/wiki/Applied_linguistics

4

TEACHER MOTIVATION

Overview

Teacher motivation is important for TESOL (Teachers of English to Speakers of Other Languages) career path development (CPD) because as we move along our career paths, we are motivated by different forces – both internal and external. In this chapter, I will address teacher motivation. While most research in motivation is about learners (beginning with the seminal work in second language acquisition by Gardner & Lambert, 1972 and later, Dörnyei, 2014; Ushioda & Dörnyei, 2009), an exploration of the role of motivation for teachers at various stages of their careers will perhaps allow us to address three areas that, until now, have been mostly ignored: (1) how teacher motivation serves teachers and students, (2) how teachers can remain motivated at different stages and throughout our careers, and (3) how to educate and prepare teachers for fulfilling careers in an ever-changing world.

We all want to have a lot of motivation. But why? What forces push us along throughout our careers as TESOL professionals? And how does that motivation work to guide us along our career paths? Why do we decide to become TESOL professionals in the first place; and what sustains us over time? How hard are we willing to work to pursue our professional work? Of course, as is the case for all aspects of our work, we are an international professional group; TESOLers worldwide aren't the same. Within any group – international, national, regional, or local – teachers vary and so does their motivation. But it seems to me, on the basis of my own experience and that of others in many countries where I've been fortunate enough to work with many TESOL professionals, our motivation plays a significant role in determining what professional choices we make.

For these reasons, I include teacher motivation as essential content in a book on TESOL CPD.

Story

One Egyptian teacher put it bluntly, "I love teaching. But I am no longer motivated: Students don't want to learn; administration fails me day in and day out with new, difficult and time-consuming tasks that have nothing to do with my own professional satisfaction nor for my students' learning; and my colleagues feel like I do: tired, burnt out and ready to quit! Without feeling motivated, we don't want to teach any more" (personal communication, February 2019).

I discovered Gardner and Lambert in 1980 and from that day until now, my interest in and commitment to an understanding of how motivation works to help students learn English continues. But in those intervening 30 years along my own career path, I have also joined many former students and colleagues to question the extent to which my own motivation, as teacher, carries weight in students' hard work. How does my motivation affect them?

Until I started working on this book, I didn't know much about teacher motivation except for what I heard from my colleagues and friends, mostly anecdotes on a professional encounter that either raised or lowered their motivation: "My boss is so great; she always notices when we pull extra hours to work on the curriculum." And a recent text message from a colleague in India: "I just got a grant to go to TESOL – yay!" Of course, there are the negative experiences where the message is one of diminished motivation: "I can't do another assessment report for the VP; he's so hard to please. I never do these right. I'd rather die!" Or "If my students don't start coming to class on time, I'm quitting." Teacher motivation is complex and interesting; and I believe it's one of the most important factors in TESOL CPD. Read on and maybe you will too.

What Is Teacher Motivation?

According to Dörnyei (2014), motivation is "responsible for *why* people decide to do something, *how long* they are willing to sustain the activity, and *how hard* they are going to pursue it" (p. 519).

In addition, Ushioda (2003) describes teacher motivation in the context of a classroom where teacher motivation has been shown to interrelate with student motivation. The teacher is a class member and must find "stimulation so that learners will discover things they want to do for themselves" (p. 10). Here, we find an overlap between teachers and students. This is a fascinating idea and one to which we'll return.

It has been a commonly held belief that the extent to which teachers are motivated determines in large part the directions we take and the choices we

44 Teacher Motivation

have in our career paths in TESOL. How does it factor into our professional lives as we move along throughout our careers? In my own experience and based on conversations with hundreds of teachers over the years, it seems that teachers' motivations are essential components of how our careers develop and progress.

What is striking is that most of what we know about teacher motivation has come to us from the research done on motivation among learners. Is teacher motivation really the same as learner motivation? Are there overlaps? A commonly held belief among teachers (and others) is that learner motivation correlates with teacher motivation – the more motivated the teacher, the more motivated the students? Perhaps Ushioda's observation (quoted above) reflects this same belief? What drives teachers to do the work we do? Do those forces driving us change at various stages of our careers – preservice, novice, mid-career, veteran, and semiretired? Few researchers have addressed teacher motivation directly.

One exception is the seminal work by Martha Pennington in 1991, reported in Ushioda and Dörnyei (2009). Pennington looks carefully at teacher autonomy in the classroom, opportunities for advancement, company policies, recognition, and working conditions. But those factors represent only a part of teacher motivation. In his 2012 dissertation, Chris Hastings looks squarely at teacher motivation in the Kingdom of Saudi Arabia. Hastings finds that money is the big motivator for teachers in his study and wonders: "What happens when the money isn't there? What motivates teachers elsewhere?" (p. 140). More research in other contexts of English language teaching is needed.

Hastings notes that there is nowhere in Pennington's survey where teachers are asked about their attitudes toward language, students, or students' language (1989, p. 11). With emphasis on the end of the 20th and beginning of the 21st centuries, Dörnyei and Ushioda situate motivation work in the context of learning English as a means of identity shift and sense of self. This presentation of work on motivation is in the context of English as the language of global communication in this era. This is most likely the context in which many of us teachers have studied and applied our knowledge on this fascinating part of language teaching. We need to know more about motivation for teachers of English to speakers of other languages.

For some researchers, teacher motivation is a worthy focus. In addition to Hastings, early research on teacher motivation (Sylvia & Hutchison, 1985) identified several important factors: social variables and collegial support positive supervisor relations; gratification from intrinsic work elements and dissatisfaction with extrinsic elements (pay and benefits); interesting work; opportunity for learning and development; negative attitude toward duties; job security, clear expectations; and excessive workloads.

Put simply, L2 motivation is currently in the process of being radically reconceptualized and retheorized in the context of contemporary notions of self and identity. This volume brings together the first comprehensive anthology of key conceptual and empirical papers that mark this important paradigmatic shift (Ushioda & Dörnyei, 2009, p. 1).

In summary, what appears to be a focus on English language learners and the learning process and teachers' attitudes about workplace issues omit the critical and complex definitions and role of teacher motivation – why and how teachers remain engaged in their professional identity development as they move ahead in their careers. Without more research on teacher motivation, we face the difficult reality that we face today: teachers who burn out and leave the profession, policies that don't address the importance of professional instruction and assessment and teacher education programs where young and novice teachers' drive to work hard and do well is, simply, not a part of the program. This approach creates underprepared teachers who are equipped with tools for excellence in instruction but whose own needs are not a part of the canon. I hope that in some way this book will address the urgent need to change this and improve our teacher education programs. In so doing, we might prepare teachers who are better at self-care; who advocate on behalf of their own professional skills, compensation, and status in institutions where they work worldwide; and who experience more job satisfaction that sustains throughout their careers.

1. How does teacher motivation change throughout our careers in TESOL? TESOL professionals, like teachers in other fields too, are committed to their students, to their programs, and to doing an excellent job, regardless of the stage at which they are in their career paths.

   In the research for my publication on "Communities of Practice" in *The TESOL Encyclopedia of English Language Teaching* (Vol. 8), teacher motivation played a significant role. TESOLers create social contexts – both face-to-face and online for professional development in order to establish opportunities for professional community membership, professional identity, and networking. In addition, ours is a unique community of practice because TESOLers operate (almost exclusively) in interdisciplinary projects, multicultural groups (including native and non-native English-speaking teacher colleagues) (England, 2018).

2. What follows are some observations of teacher motivation and behaviors and habits at different stages of their careers.

   Teachers' behaviors and habits are to some extent based on their motivation: What makes us teach the way we do at different phases of our careers? In different cultural contexts? Work contexts? And in so doing, how do we avoid burnout, a challenge at all stages of our careers (see Coombe, England, & Schmidt, 2012, for a variety of approaches to addressing burnout).

Preservice teachers are often motivated by classroom-based projects for which they can try out using their newly acquired knowledge and skills.

46 Teacher Motivation

Supervised practicum experiences offer opportunities to open the door for teachers to do what motivates them by tapping into their first stage of career motivation. These early experiences can be critical experiences, or "career milestones," that provide models and a tone for teachers as they move ahead in their careers.

Novice/beginner teachers are more focused on doing a good job than on taking care of themselves; their work assignments may need control and limiting due a tendency for them to take on too much. Focused teaching assignments, research projects, and service offerings are better than disparate ones for novice teachers.

Mid-career/career switchers: What motivates mid-career teachers and career switchers is often money, what is called "an extrinsic motivator." While mid-career teachers are motivated for professional enhancement, increasing numbers of teachers are leaving TESOL, ESL (English as a Second Language), and EFL (English as a Foreign Language) in favor of higher paying jobs or those with more job security and benefits. TESOL International Association membership numbers have decreased significantly over the past decade, though have leveled off in recent years. In addition, considering the role of research in a teacher's career, mid-career teachers are likely motivated to develop their research skills. Career switchers bring skills and knowledge from prior workplaces to their work in English as a second language and English as a foreign language teaching. English language programs benefit from career switcher employees in a variety of ways. In some settings, these programs are able to build new niche markets. In one program, two attorneys who completed TESOL training programs were able to establish an international program in legal English writing, now a model for English for legal purposes in our field. It was the combined expertise and motivation of these career switchers – now with law and TESOL skills and knowledge – that made the program excellent.

Veteran teachers: These teachers are likely those with a number of years of service, in which they have acquired skills and knowledge and status to be "top earners." They are committed to excellence and they rely on their procedural knowledge to drive their work lives. Motivated by the desire to maintain some professional identity and, at the same time, to move into less-than-full workdays, veteran teachers are excellent mentors and role models.

Semiretired teachers: While some semiretired teachers like to do part-time teaching, many choose to work with volunteer programs (at home or elsewhere worldwide). Motivation is to feel needed, to contribute, and to maintain a sense of work identity acquired during their careers. According to Nicholson (2018), we get more into internal purposes as we age, who puts it like this: we "renunciate externally anchored purposes" in favor of intrinsic motivations and drive: helping others, addressing an activity we consider meaningful and sustaining.

Summary and Next Steps and How to Stay Motivated!

Motivation among TESOL professionals is present throughout our careers. What sources we see as those that keep us going (or "stay motivated") will vary depending on the stage we are in our careers. What worked when we were starting out may not be the same motivation we need as we move forward.

Professional networks are essential to motivation at all stages. And teachers are individually predisposed/gifted at acquiring a good network. Our networks – colleagues, mentors, and friends – help us to stay engaged and connected with others. And that is true throughout our careers. The extent to which we have acquired a professional group of fellow teachers, researchers, authors, and professional and community service providers can motivate us.

Professional success can also be highly motivating. Does motivation lead to success or does success in teaching make us more motivated? The better we do, the more we want to do it. In a recent blog post, Quy (2018) offered the following insight on the extent to which success can "lull us into complacency." And it is this complacency that can empower us to move on to a new job, a next phase of our career paths or, in rare cases, to leaving the field altogether. Check it out at this link: https://www.smartbrief.com/original/2018/10/why-success-alone-doesnt-mean-youve-made-real-progress?utm_source=brief

In summary, our (teachers') motivation is a key feature in our TESOL career paths. In the words of Susan Fowler (2018), "motivation is contagious when we choose to live our values." We create positive energy for ourselves – and for others around us, students, and colleagues alike – when we make choices that apply our values and motivation to our work and lives. When we strive to better ourselves through hard work and learning new skills, we do create that energy.

Recommendations

When we speak of teacher motivation in the context of TESOL, we are connecting our own passions and drive to that of others. It is pretty clear from the analysis above that teacher motivation changes – ebbs and flows and adjusts its focus – at various stages of our TESOL careers. Often, those "others" are our students. Sometimes, they are colleagues. Almost always, those "others" are supervisors. How do others judge me? How do I compare with others? How am I performing relative to my own expectations of the required standards? Which identity is most important to me at this time? Research in emotional labor indicates the need to look more deeply into teacher motivation as it relates to CPD. In their seminal work, Ashforth and Humphrey (1993) provide some potentially

48 Teacher Motivation

valuable definitions for those seeking to better understand teacher motivation and its role in TESOL CPD:

> *Emotional labor* is the display of expected emotions by service agents during service encounters. It is performed through surface acting, deep acting, or the expression of genuine emotion. Emotional labor may facilitate task effectiveness and self-expression, but it also may prime customer expectations that cannot be met and may trigger emotive dissonance and self-alienation. However, following social identity theory, we argue that some effects of emotional labor are moderated by one's social and personal identities and that emotional labor stimulates pressures for the person to identify with the service role. (p. 88)

More research and better definition of TESOL teacher motivation is required – both as it affects learners and learning and importantly, how teachers experience motivational impact on their career path decision-making and employment trajectory.

References

Ashforth, B. E., & R. H. Humphrey (1993). Emotional labor in service roles: The influence of identity. *Academy of Management Review, 8*(1). Retrieved from https://doi.org/10.5465/amr.1993.3997508

Coombe, C., England, L., & Schmidt, J. (2012). *Reigniting, retooling, and retiring in English language teaching.* Ann Arbor, MI: University of Michigan Press. Retrieved from https://shenandoah.on.worldcat.org/oclc/741023752

Dörnyei, Z. (2014). Motivation in second language learning. In M. Celce-Murcia, D. Brinton, M. A. Snow, & D. Bohlke (Eds.), *Teaching English as a second or foreign language* (4th ed.). Boston, MA: Cengage Learning.

England, L. (2018). Communities of practice. In J. I. Liontas (ed.), *The TESOL encyclopedia of English language teaching* (Vol. 8). New York, NY: Wiley-Blackwell Publishers. doi.org/10.1002/9781118784235.eelt0396.

Fowler, S. (2018). How to generate positive energy (weblog comment). Retrieved from https://www.smartbrief.com/original/2018/10/how-generate-positive-energy

Gardner, R. C., & Lambert, W. E. (1972). *Attitudes and motivation in second language learning.* Rowley, MA: Newbury House Publishers.

Hastings, C. J. (2012). *Attitudes & acculturation: A qualitative case study of EFL teachers in Saudi Arabia* (unpublished dissertation). TN: The University of Memphis.

Nicholson, N. (2018, October 10). What's the point of purpose? London Business School Review. Retrieved from https://www.london.edu/faculty-and-research/lbsr/whats-the-point-of-purpose

Pennington, M. C. (1989). Directions for faculty evaluation in language education. *Language, Culture and Curriculum, 2*(3), 167. https://doi.org/10.1080/07908318909525064

Quy, L. (2018, October 17). Why success alone doesn't mean you've made real progress (Web log comment). Retrieved from https://www.smartbrief.com/original/2018/10/why-success-alone-doesnt-mean-youve-made-real-progress?utm_source=brief

Sylvia, R. D., & Hutchison, T. (1985). What makes Ms. Johnson teach? A study of teacher motivation. *Human Relations*. https://doi.org/10.1177/001872678503800902

Ushioda, E. (2003). Motivation as a socially mediated process. In D. Little, J. Ridley, & E. Ushioda (Eds.), *Learner autonomy in the foreign language classroom: Teacher, learner, curriculum and assessment*. Dublin, Ireland: Authentik Language Learning Resources Ltd. Retrieved from https://www.researchgate.net/profile/David_Little2/publication/317264706_Learner_autonomy_in_the_foreign_language_classroom_teacher_learner_curriculum_and_assssment/links/592ed1eea6fdcc89e76992c0/Learner-autonomy-in-the-foreign-language-classroom-teacher-learner-curriculum-and-assssment.pdf#page=98

Ushioda, E., & Dörnyei, Z. (2009). *Motivation, language identity and the L2 self*. Bristol, UK: Multilingual Matters. Retrieved from http://search.ebscohost.com/login.aspx?direct=true&db=nlebk&AN=245456&site=bsi-live

5

ORGANIZATIONAL DEVELOPMENT

Background

How and to what extent does an organization influence a TESOL (Teachers of English to Speakers of Other Languages) career path? How do organizations support teachers in their efforts to create communities of practice, networking, and completion of complex collaborative projects in their cross-disciplinary, multicultural (including native and non-native speaking teacher colleagues and students) workplaces? (See more on the foundations and structure of communities of practice in England, 2018). These are questions I will address in this chapter.

For purposes here, organizations refer to any group or body of people with a particular purpose such as a school, university, a society, or association. According to the *Encyclopedia of Management* by Augier and Teece (2018), a definition for organizational development is as follows.

Organizational development is an ongoing, systematic process to implement effective change in an organization. Organizational development is known as both a field of applied behavioral science focused on understanding and managing organizational change and as a field of scientific study and inquiry. It is interdisciplinary in nature and draws on sociology, psychology, and theories of motivation, learning, and personality.

Story

With a successful career teaching English, a former student (here, I'll call her "M") accepted several promotions in the university Intensive English Program (IEP) she had joined about 20 years ago. Having been a popular teacher, brought in innovative programming, recruited large numbers of students, and acquired accreditation from an internationally recognized body; IEP became one of the fastest growing and most sought after in the United States under M's leadership. Her career path was progressive and successful. She was named Program Director several years ago. On a regular workday recently, M returned to her desk after lunch, opened her university computer as usual and discovered that she had been locked out. Assuming it was an example of an outdated password or some similar technical glitch, M checked in with her boss, the dean. The dean asked her to go with him to Human Resources, where she was informed that she was terminated. In the days that followed, the details of her termination became somewhat clearer, with a description of a three-month severance package and the explanation that the reason for her termination was that enrollment projections were very low. In the course of a few minutes, M's life as an employed, successful, and senior TESOL professional turned into unemployment. "In a second, my whole life changed" (personal communication, January 7, 2019).

With apologies for the weightiness of the story I've selected to open this chapter, it is hardly "fake news" that such experiences are frequently heard these days. As political and economic forces bear down harder than ever on education programs in the United States and worldwide, TESOL professionals at all levels and in all geographical areas face the increasing possibility of being "fired" or "let go" without much warning.

We need to change the ways in which we view "job security." Loyalty and commitment are one thing; but for many programs, numbers count and dwindling enrollments create challenges for those who represent the interests of TESOLers. While tenure and contracts can help, many TESOLers now and for the future face new challenges in addressing the ways in which we see organizations and the ways in which they change and evolve. This chapter will help us in that effort.

For TESOLers, it is not only to ourselves as professionals we must look in order to address a better understanding of our career path development. We are individuals, but we function professionally inside of organizations. And that relationship – between individual TESOL professionals and the organizations with which we are associated – is becoming increasingly complex. For our purposes in this chapter, those are two organizations: (1) organizations that hire and train us, "places of employment," and (2) professional associations that represent our interests. These two types of organizations are essential to our understanding of career paths development for TESOLers; and in this chapter, we will address the extent to which the successes and shortcomings of organizational structures affect our career paths.

Successes and Shortcomings of Organizations That Hire Us

Places of employment invest somewhat in individuals, but in most instances, those efforts include ways of developing and promoting the identity of the organization – the university, school, government/ministries, or company – not

52 Organizational Development

the individual teacher. This focus on organizational identity is a shortcoming when it omits investment in individual teachers as employees.

In an early description of organizational development, Margulies and Raia (1972) offered three components: planned change, organizational learning, and consultation. Depending on where we are on our career paths, these components will influence us differently. And organizations need to address the professional needs of teachers. How can schools, universities, ministries and corporate employers support teachers' individual career paths?

Further reading and in-depth analysis of organizational development are available in a number of sources, including the seminal publication by Jones and Brazzel (2014).

The familiar model of teacher as employee often includes emphasis on evaluation. Drawing on teaching abilities, research productivity, and service (to the profession and to the community), academic programs of study evaluate performance. For most programs, a collection of all faculty teaching, research, and service contributes to the quality, reputation, and size of the program. Plans for change are made in line with and to the extent to which faculty performance contributes to the quality, reputation, and size of the student body. Organizationally sponsored professional development programs are often offered by program administration in order to promote the development of new knowledge and additional and/or updated skills for faculty and staff. And consultants are hired to provide "an outside perspective" on ways in which organizational change might be needed. For TESOL, organizational development includes additional factors, including cultural and linguistic diversity. While internal audits and accreditation-based documentation are internally and confidentially generated, more research is needed on English language teacher education and English language programs' organizational development.

I suggest that the approach to address organizational development in TESOL settings should be revised to focus less on how these organization-sponsored activities influence the institution or workplace and how teacher-focused professional development might be carried out. In addition, teachers might also be more intentional in their effect on teachers' careers, whether those are in the same or a different institutional setting. Some excellent professional workplace settings in colleges, universities, and schools already do these: How can I use my annual teaching evaluation to get a promotion in my current program? Or get a job elsewhere? Can I use my work on the curriculum project (or assessment, accreditation, placement procedures – fill in the blank) in my current job to improve my job security in my current position? In another institution? Are my research and publications considered legitimate in another college, university, or school? And how do my service activities help me to promote myself professionally in- and outside my current workplace? With an emphasis on teachers, not on institutions in which they are employed, we may find better, happier teachers whose professional needs are met more directly and more intentionally than in traditional work settings. More detail appears in Chapter 10 of this volume on the subject of intentionalizing our TESOL career path development.

In addition to on-the-job training and professional development within one's employment workplace, professional development for TESOL professionals often occurs in the context of a TESOL professional association: TESOL International Association or one of its (approximately) hundred affiliates (115 according to TESOL Executive Director, Christopher Powers, 2019), International Association of Teachers of English as a Foreign Language (IATEFL) and its associates, among other regional, state/provincial, and other organizations. The choices for these grows every day.

In the next section, I will briefly describe three contexts in which I have found English language teachers at all career path stages to have professional development opportunities: (1) TESOL and IATEFL (in general these are the two widely known professional associations though others are being organized and regularly appear on social media); (2) TESOL affiliates; and (3) what I will call "seat of their pants" – where groups and individuals create their own non-association-affiliated professional development programming.

Successes and Shortcomings of Professional Organizations We Join

In professional associations, efforts are made to promote and maintain professional excellence.

Members are given many opportunities through professional association membership, whether in an international, national, regional, or local affiliate. While in its infancy, research on language teacher associations is an important aspect of TESOL career path development. Still, it is clear that these associations provide opportunities for professional growth, learning, and development. See Elsheikh, Coombe, and Effiong (2018) for a first-ever collection of scholarly work on English language teacher associations.

Indeed, it is fair to say that TESOL professional associations are among the most significant influences on one's professional career path development. My own professional identity may be of interest: I have early career experiences as an affiliate member, then a leader (followed by and concomitant with a number of international association leadership roles). And dozens of my former students (and in some cases their students!) make me a "mother" and "grandmother" of TESOL leaders worldwide at all levels – local, regional, national, and international. It is in no small part *because of* the TESOL International Association structure that I (and many like me) have known extraordinary professional success in TESOL – even now as I am comfortably in the "semiretired stage!"

54 Organizational Development

In our coauthored chapter in a recent book entitled *The Role of Language Teacher Associations in Professional Development* (edited by Elsheikh, Coombe, and Effiong), Mahboob and I have addressed "Reality and potential: English language teacher associations in the 21st century" (2018, pp. 25–38). The chapter details how and to what extent language teacher associations address the professional development needs of teachers throughout their careers. There is indeed much to be done to realize the potential of these organizations in improving the quality of English language teachers' professional lives worldwide.

TESOL and IATEFL

TESOL International Association (n.d.) mission statement puts it this way, "TESOL International Association advances the expertise of professionals who teach English to speakers of other languages in multilingual contexts worldwide. We accomplish this through professional learning, research, standards, & advocacy."

While "& advocacy" would suggest attention to the TESOL member's professional career path development, most of TESOL's advocacy efforts reflect a commitment to students served by teachers and the intersection between teachers and students (what I'll call "the learning process and/or experience"), not advocacy on behalf of teachers, themselves.

IATEFL (n.d.) also has a mission statement as follows:

> "Our mission (is) to 'link, develop and support English Language Teaching professionals worldwide.'" And its "wider mission" brings IATEFL to a bigger audience beyond the reach of traditional, face-to-face conferences and events to its associates as follows:
>
> Our wider mission: In addition to meeting the professional development needs of its members, IATEFL helps to serve the needs of the wider ELT community through: an online live-streaming of our annual conference open to all (60,000 plus audience); making our monthly webinars and annual web conferences available to non-members; many of our SIG discussion forums and webinars being open to all; an open social media site with over 12,000 members; IATEFL Projects and joint training awards open to other teacher associations an expanding scholarship programme, so that deserving teachers can become active in our annual conference, SIG events and online courses; and practical assistance to those who want to establish their own local Teachers' Associations.

In their recently published book, the first (to my knowledge) on the topic of professional associations, Elsheikh, Coombe and Effiong (2018) have presented a first-ever effort to provide detailed analysis of how language teacher associations work. In addition to other sources, please see reference to selected chapters in this volume as I address professional associations below.

Unfortunately, TESOL International Association membership is open only to those who can afford it. While there are deep discounts for those on limited incomes (or for those who don't have institutional support for membership fees), not all English teachers are able to join TESOL International Association nor can all English teachers take advantage of TESOL's member-only professional development resources. In addition, the Annual Convention, the signature TESOL International Association event, is always held in the United States; and it is available only to those who can fund a trip to the city where the convention is held. For many teachers, TESOL Convention attendance is barely a vague dream; for others (very likely the majority of teachers of English worldwide), the Annual TESOL International Association Convention is quite simply unknown. TESOL International Association offers ongoing web-based professional development programs, available to members. Ongoing efforts are made by the TESOL staff to provide useful programs to help improve member engagement. IATEFL, founded in the United Kingdom, has a smaller membership than TESOL International, but is well-established with a strong positive reputation worldwide, an annual conference, and many opportunities for professional development throughout the year.

1. TESOL affiliate members have access to professional development opportunities. Numbering approximately 100, TESOL affiliates welcome thousands of members in specified geographical regions (often national but also regional groups). While precise numbers of affiliate members are difficult to ascertain, the work of TESOL affiliates reflects the diversity, complexity, and efforts of extraordinary individuals, most of whom are volunteers. IATEFL associates sustain a similar program of offerings.
2. Finally, the largest group of all are the perhaps millions of English teachers worldwide who have no professional association affiliation.

In the story that opens this chapter, might M's professional association membership have supported her during the run-up, "the day of" and the follow-up to her being fired? Do professional organizations have an obligation to members as they experience shortfalls in recruitment and enrollment numbers and other factors for which they, the members, have no real direct responsibility? I would say they do.

How Organizations Influence TESOL Career Paths

Professional organizations promote excellence in teaching and research. In some narrowly defined projects, they advocate for some members, national policies having impact on English language learning and learners, and other specifically

56 Organizational Development

selected issues. But addressing teachers' needs, specifically, seems to be a side interest. Drawing on M's story above, there is little question that her employer influenced her career path. She was fired unexpectedly due to enrollment decreases. However, because of her long period of service and the network she had created statewide and internationally, M's options were more varied than those for others who were let go from the same program.

M had established herself as a leader in her local TESOL affiliate; she had recruited students worldwide and had friends "in high places" both in her home state and in a number of countries from which she had recruited students. In addition, her colleagues in other departments on campus knew her well and were at the ready to support her efforts in finding a new position. So, with the efforts of both her university and the professional affiliate community, M has high hopes for future employment. And it was in the organization for which she had been working (for 20 years) that she had acquired those resources.

The organizational structure supported M's professional development throughout her employment there. With strong records of excellence in teaching, some research-based publications and professional leadership service (at the university level on campus committees and with her TESOL affiliate) and service to the community (as a volunteer), M personifies the consummate "TESOL professional." And it was at her own hand that she had acquired that record; but it was also because of the strength of her university organization that she had developed those skills and (now) valuable resources for her next career steps.

Super (1980) introduces the importance of home, community, and school as "theaters" to describe the importance of context in career path development. Places of employment provide teachers with "theaters," or contexts of work. And the ways in which these function are essential to job satisfaction and productivity. I will add to this discussion that organizations in TESOL – whether workplaces or professional associations – include increasingly more online TESOL teacher education and professional workplaces and professional association work done virtually. This fact means that our relationships with organizations in both categories are rapidly changing.

For preservice teachers, graduate-level teacher education program (Master's in TESOL) are our "places of employment." These provide a foundational experience in the unique environment of working with colleagues in TESOL. Through course work, practical training experiences, readings, and individual and group assignments, TESOL master's candidates begin their careers with a "theater" with whom they are "actors," addressing superiors (their professors), colleagues (fellow master's candidates in their programs), and English language learners (with whom they work as practicum students). In addition, candidates complete theses, capstone course projects, and other research-based requirements.

Organizational Development **57**

It is in these preservice settings that TESOL professionals acquire their professional identities, learn to work with professors, colleagues, and students. The organization of the graduate academic program creates a foundation for our career paths. Professional expectations are established in those programs and those carry with us throughout our careers. When a veteran teacher, such as is described above in my story of M, experiences the termination news as delivered, it's a bit of a shock because, as she put it, "I had never previously had such an experience and I haven't ever hired nor fired someone in such a way" (personal communication, January 7, 2019).

Here, I have presented a short anecdote on how preservice organizational structures influence TESOLers at the beginnings of our careers, an in-depth analysis of ways in which the organizational development characteristics of our places of employment influence us throughout the five stages of our careers? With myriad factors influencing the "theater," there is rich ground here for research on how organizations influence our careers. For now, I have provided a list of timely research questions for interested readers to consider.

What organizational efforts are made to help teachers move forward on their career paths?

Places of employment: With its emphasis on "ongoing, systematic processes" for change, organizational development focuses naturally on the organization, not on the individual teacher. How do workplaces influence TESOL career path development? What aspects of M's earlier career path prepared her well for what was to come? How can graduate-level teacher education prepare new teachers with the knowledge and skills and intentional use of those in addressing career path development? How can we help teachers like M to acquire the knowledge and skills that might allow them to avoid feeling like victims and in some cases, actually being victimized by organizations that fail to support them or even harm them? And how can we all learn from the stories of our colleagues, like M, who must "retool for the next milestone" in our careers?

Professional associations: Through their annual conventions, publications, and live and recorded electronic streaming efforts, both IATEFL and TESOL make heroic efforts to reach out to teacher members to help them to be better teachers. Affiliates of TESOL and associates in IATEFL all do the same. What is lacking is a support system for teachers to navigate their career paths in ways that allow teachers opportunities to celebrate their own and one another's successes and to survive when times are hard and the chips are down. More efforts are needed to address the needs of teachers at various stages in their careers. Based on communications over the years with a variety of colleagues, former students and mentees, there is extreme need for more support for teachers throughout their careers. Here are a few suggestions: What can associations (and their smaller affiliates or associates) do to help teachers – preservice teachers who want to get involved? Novice teachers in order to help them to contribute effectively? How

58 Organizational Development

might the professional development needs of novice teachers differ from the needs of a career switcher or veteran teacher? And what skills do veteran teachers need in order to prepare for semiretirement?

Interaction between places of employment and professional associations: How and to what extent might workplace organizations (schools, colleges, and universities) work with professional associations to support teachers as they move along in their careers? How might an ideal relationship look – between places of employment and professional associations in TESOL – help us along our career paths? I will close this chapter with some suggestions to move forward with ideas to address these questions and others.

TESOL career path development is about managing change. As my meditation teacher puts it so well, "Keep calm knowing change." It's a good idea. Try it!

How can we be engaged and happy with relentless worries and threats of replacement of full-time faculty with adjuncts and no benefits? How can we deal with threats of downsizing, less pay than in the past, increasing workloads, and bigger class sizes? How can we stay ahead and learn the instructional technology skills needed for the diverse, complex, and ever-changing use of online platforms (perceived by administration as cheaper than face-to-face models)? And how do we combat the extraordinary outsourcing of teaching, materials and assessment tools, and other functions previously owned by teachers? How can we be satisfied with our jobs? And how can we go about advocating for ourselves without the benefit of theory and policy that informs our practice as we move through our careers? These struggles are no less for TESOLers than for other teacher specialties.

The best way to address these issues is to identify, design, and implement an intentional plan for our own career path development. Discomfort is the price of admission to a meaningful life. Knowing that change is around us, we have tools at our disposal already; we can add a new teaching or research skill, change a habit, buy a new laptop or take an exercise class. We can be the masters and mistresses of our own destinies! We can start today with our workplaces and our professional associations. And we can move beyond those as well.

Organizations serve TESOL career path development – one way or the other. Workplace-based environments make us want to work hard, learn more, and experience the sense of joy and satisfaction that we all seek on the job. Or they can kill us – physically, mentally, and/or spiritually. At the same time, professional associations can help us to be professionally rejuvenated, to retool with new knowledge and skills, and to build our professional networks. And like workplaces, professional associations can drag us down. There are other ways of organizations to support teachers – other than what we see today. Chapter 9 contains some ideas for organizations to support TESOL professionals throughout our careers.

References

Augier, M., & Teece, D. J. (2018). *The Palgrave encyclopedia of strategic management living edition.* London, UK: Palgrave Macmillan.

Elsheikh, A., Coombe, C., & Effiong, O. (Eds.). (2018). *The role of language teacher associations in professional development.* Cham, Switzerland: Springer. https://doi.org/10.1007/978-3-030-00967-0

England, L. (2018). Communities of practice. In J. I. Liontas (Ed.), *The TESOL encyclopedia of English language teaching* (Vol. 8). New York, NY: Wiley-Blackwell. https://doi.org/10.1002/9781118784235.eelt0396

IATEFL. (n.d.). IATEFL's mission, goals and practices (PDF file). Retrieved from https://members.iatefl.org/downloads/member_info/IATEFL_mission_goals_practices.pdf

Jones, B. B., & Brazzel, M. (2014). *NTL institute handbook of organizational development and change: Principles, practices and perspectives* (2nd ed.). San Francisco, CA: Wiley, on behalf of NTL.

Mahboob, A., & England, L. (2018). Reality and potential: English language teacher associations in the 21st century. In A. Elsheikh, C. Coombe, & O. Effiong (Eds.), *The role of language teacher associations in professional development* (pp. 25–38). New York: Springer. https://www.springer.com/us/book/9783030009663

Margulies, N., & Raia, A. P. (1972). *Organizational development: Values, process, and technology.* New York, NY: McGraw-Hill Book Company.

Powers, C. (2019, March 15). Presentation at TESOL International Association Convention Annual Business Meeting, Atlanta, GA.

Super, D. E. (1980). A life-span, life-space approach to career development. *Journal of Vocational Behavior, 16*(3), 282–298.

TESOL International Association. (n.d.). Mission and values (PDF file). Retrieved from https://www.tesol.org/about-tesol/association-governance/mission-and-values

6
LEADERSHIP

Overview

As I write this chapter on TESOL (Teaching English to Speakers of Other Languages) leadership, I am sitting in a university library in the United States where all the news is on a gaping leadership crisis in this country. For the first time in history, we have no real leadership: no Secretary of Defense, no White House Chief of Staff, no Attorney General, no one is sure who's running the Department of Justice, the stock market is crashing, and the federal government is on the verge of being shut down entirely. America is in crisis. And this doesn't include the Russia investigation and all that is following in February. But TESOL is not the US government, thankfully. TESOL is a non-profit organization bound by the terms of that designation. As a profession and an academic discipline, TESOL has leadership: Through our established professional communities, we are fortunate indeed to have hundreds of individuals worldwide who lead by example, who care about our profession, and who give of their time and treasure to maintain high standards of professional activity in academic institutions where we work and in professional associations that are designed to support us.

And still, my focus on leadership in TESOL career path development is particularly relevant today. Many countries face leadership crises (not so different from those I described above in the United States); and professional groups do too. All of us function as part of "teams" and so those who lead are essential to our careers. Good leaders impact our careers and our career paths in international, national, regional, and local contexts. TESOL isn't government; but leadership is important at all levels as we progress in our careers.

What we don't know well is how leadership skills evolve, change, and are sought after in making policy and advocating on our behalf outside the profession. Governments, nongovernmental agencies, scholarship, and exchange programs support TESOL professionals throughout our professional careers; but how do they view our value and our professional efforts in teaching, research, and service? I hope to shed some light on these and other TESOL leadership issues as those relate to career path development in this chapter.

In their article on "10 roles of teacher leaders," Harrison and Killion (2007) identified the following. These may be a close approximation for TESOL leaders too: resource provider, instructional specialist, curriculum specialist, classroom supporter, learning facilitator, mentor, school leader, data coach, catalyst for change, and learner. We will return to this list in Chapter 10.

What Is Teacher Leadership in TESOL?

According to the Association for Supervision and Curriculum Development (ASCD), teacher leadership includes particularly well-developed knowledge, skills, and passion for work; and it starts when teachers have influence outside of their classrooms. Here's a quotation from ASCD's web-based documents:

> The term teacher leadership refers to that set of skills demonstrated by teachers who continue to teach students but also have an influence that extends beyond their own classrooms to others within their own school and elsewhere. It entails mobilizing and energizing others with the goal of improving the school's performance of its critical responsibilities related to teaching and learning. Mobilizing and energizing does not occur because of the role of the leader as boss (as might be the case with a principal), but rather because the individual is informed and persuasive. Therefore, an important characteristic of a teacher leader is expertise and skill in engaging others in complex work. It also entails an unwavering passion for the core mission of the school and the courage to confront obstacles to achieving that mission.
>
> Because improvement of a school's performance frequently involves doing things differently from how they have been done in the past, teacher leadership often requires managing a process of change. But this is not always the case. Many times, improvement occurs when teacher leaders motivate colleagues to become more skilled and thoughtful regarding their work, encouraging them not to do things differently but to do them *better*. At other times, of course, teacher leaders recognize an opportunity to institute a practice that will improve the school's program. In those situations, teacher leadership does require convincing others to use a new approach, but the change process involved is not that of implementing a

62 Leadership

new program, in which the stages of concern have been well documented (Loucks-Horsley, 1996). Rather, it is a professional exploration of practice. (What is Teacher Leadership, n.d.)

However, when we address a specific context, and here it's TESOL, teacher leadership is somewhat different. TESOL International Association offers a certificate and here's a description of its content and method of delivery (taken from the TESOL website):

> The Leadership Development Certificate Program (LDCP) provides quality professional development and leadership training for current or future leaders within TESOL International Association. The 40-hour self-paced online program is open to *TESOL members only*. The LDCP also benefits current or future leaders of other English language teacher associations. To make the LDCP accessible to TESOL members worldwide, it is offered online only. LDCP graduates are also able to participate in additional networking opportunities on leadership issues. (TESOL Leadership, n.d.)

Focused squarely on the "leadership training for current or future leaders within TESOL International Association," emphasis for this certificate program is less on teachers than it is on the needs of the professional association. Hopefully, there is some overlap between those!

And in a rare international approach to research on teacher leadership, Amzat and Valdez (2017) have published reports from researchers and practitioners across borders with an emphasis on theoretical arguments and empirical data on teacher empowerment. This book shows well how teachers are ready to improve their own professional skills from the point of view of various stakeholders. These finds are in direct conflict with the often held belief that teachers are unable or unwilling to change. Given empowerment tools, according to these researchers, teachers do indeed change – willingly.

Because TESOL career paths are exceptionally diverse in the ways in which leadership knowledge and skills are acquired and used, this chapter begins not with one but with three "Stories." I hope readers will be able to connect with these stories and to write their own.

Story 1: "Forced Leadership Training"

My own professional career path was greatly influenced by what might best be described as "forced leadership training." Early on, in graduate school, I was one among some fortunate graduate student colleagues in a large university environment where there were world class scholars teaching and conducting research across campus. It was common to learn that one or another faculty member had been awarded an internationally recognized symbol of professional success – Nobel Prizes, MacArthur Foundation Grants, many Fulbright teaching and research awards, National Endowment for the Humanities awards, and more. In short, we graduate students were surrounded by high achievers. And we too were given the tools and were expected to achieve. In our first semesters, we were pushed (hard) to find a topic about which we had passion. Then, we were to write a proposal and submit the proposal for consideration on the TESOL affiliate or TESOL International Association, American Association of Applied Linguistics, or some other professional conference program. For those lucky ones among us whose proposals were accepted, we were then faced with the next challenge – applying for travel money. When my proposal was accepted for TESOL 1982 (you may recall that the international conference was in Honolulu; and did I mention that my graduate school was located in Urbana, Illinois?), I was in the unenviable position of (a) having to accept the invitation to present the paper because to have rejected it would have been professional suicide; and (b) following my academic advisor's (not) suggestion (but "order") to call the dean and ask him for the plane fare. "What?" asked the dean when I explained I wanted money to attend and present at a professional conference. "Honolulu? Our graduate students don't go to Honolulu!" Well, he did give me the plane fare and I did go to Honolulu for my first-ever TESOL International Convention conference presentation. Leadership skills – that's how you learn them: You ask for something you don't think you'll ever be allowed to have and then you get it. And to this day, I still don't believe how lucky I was that that dean knew exactly what he was doing. Today – more than 30 years later – I'm writing about him in a book. Wow.

There are as many TESOL career paths to leadership as there are TESOL leaders. Here is one (what might be called "traditional") path. Notice how the trajectory is upward. This is one way that some of our career paths have gone in TESOL. There are many others!

Story 2: "Up, Up, and Up Again!" Job Promotion and Leadership

The following is what I hope will be a familiar description of many TESOLers' leadership experiences: We start out as teachers (could be K-12, intensive English program in a college or university, or maybe a career switcher "trainer" in another field). We move into teacher training and/or teacher education ("training" here as "on-the-job training" or perhaps "informal training") ("education" is in a more formalized degree or certificate teacher education role). We move then to "trainer of trainer," supported by forward-looking administrators who see our skills and knowledge as contributors to excellence in an academic, government, or other institutional setting. And finally, we move into "administration" (see Tannacito (2013) for a readable account aptly entitled "What, Me? An Administrator?"). Administration is attractive for many TESOL professionals because of the pay check difference: administrators, in most cases, make a lot more than teachers. So even for those who prefer teaching, administration is a next step in our career paths because of the financial benefits.

Story 3: "Another TESOL Leader Career Path Story:" Cathy Gomez

Cathy provides us with what for many of us might be a familiar description of how both TESOL professional and scholarly educational experiences combine with what might be described as "real world" experiences, acquired outside of the English language classroom, in this case, from working in a hotel restaurant. Figure 6.1 illustrates Cathy's career path.

TESOL career path phases: Here, I will provide a description of leadership skills that might be considered a part of the five stages of a TESOL career path (see Table 6.1). While intended to be neither all-encompassing nor inclusive of every single TESOL context, this chart is a good starting point for those seeking to think more deeply (and hopefully to conduct research) on leadership in TESOL.

As you consider your own career path stage or that of a family member, colleague, or friend, at which stage are you as a TESOL leader and in which roles are you serving?

It is perhaps leadership that troubles me most in TESOL. In too many instances, I have spent a great deal of my time as a TESOL professional addressing weaknesses, lack of vision, extreme lack of ethics, or other sources of failure in leadership. Having heard stories from others, read research on leadership in a variety of professional and academic disciplines, I offer the following proposal for renewing ourselves and our profession for the leadership we need for the future. As an organizational scheme, I will use the TESOL Summit 2017 list of

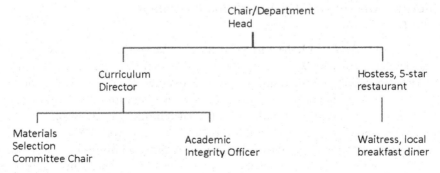

FIGURE 6.1 Cathy's career path.

Leadership **65**

TABLE 6.1 Characteristics of TESOL leaders and leadership

	Knowledge about leadership	*Skills using knowledge about leadership*	*Focus for leadership development*
Preservice	Guided by mentors; value of knowledge over experience; personal/interpersonal skills focus.	Tech savvy; strong emphasis on acquiring knowledge; refers to knowledge in addressing leadership tasks.	Peer mentoring, managing cross-cultural leadership.
Novice-beginner	Content focus; value of combined knowledge and experience.	Combines knowledge with experience in balance; lacks some knowledge to lead.	Building confidence in leadership roles.
Mid-career/career switcher	Teaching focus; draws on experience and reads and applies research seamlessly to guide leadership tasks.	Autonomous, but sometimes struggles with "boss" and can lack confidence.	Addressing diverse and sometimes leadership roles.
Veteran	Has established and publicly acknowledged leadership style and skills.	Confident leadership style and skills with specific leadership role preferences.	Learning to select leadership tasks (how to say "no"); addressing requests for mentoring former students and colleagues.
Semi-retired	A strong knowledge base – acquired over time; has varied and diverse background knowledge.	Pulls back from some leadership tasks and focuses on one or two.	Keeping up with current research and "letting go."

themes: futurology, English in multilingualism, reimagining English competence, and the profession as change agent.

The TESOL Summit 2017 was an international meeting held in Greece, during which TESOL professionals joined to address the future of our profession. You can read more about that event at this web address: https://www.tesol.org/summit-2017

We take that role in the classroom and beyond the classroom too. We in TESOL admire leaders with integrity and moral courage. TESOLers have more or less agreed that teachers are leaders. Teachers seem to fail in the fourth theme, as change agents. How do we help teachers to move beyond theory to policy and practice? How can teachers be leaders and thereby change what happens in the world of English language teaching and learning? In her paper at TESOL

66 Leadership

Convention 2018, Misty Adoniou describes how this happens: Adoniou says that guided by a structure including three lenses including micro (work of teachers in their classrooms), meso (systems in which teachers work; I call these "workplaces"), and macro (society in which teachers and systems operate). Everyone in the meso and macro systems rely on those in the micro system to tell them how to address complex issues in teaching English (Adoniou, 2019).

Here is a list of opportunities for TESOL leaders as change agents:

1. Influencing policy makers
2. Engaging effectively in debates as informed, reasonable participants
3. Pressuring teacher associations to represent their interests
4. Acquiring the language of advocacy: how do we make a difference?
5. Providing community members – parents, employers, and other professional groups – with reliable, timely information about teaching and learning (Adoniou, 2019)

And finally, how might TESOL professionals address these opportunities at various stages of our career paths? How might they better develop knowledge and skills and actually do this advocacy work as leaders – to help others in the community in addressing their goals for change?

We need more information on how and to what extent our ESL program alumni contribute to their professions and their workplaces. In addition, we need more information on how and to what extent we, teachers, make a difference/have an impact on our communities – local, regional, national, and international.

Recommendations

Teachers are, according to Brown (2010), "our most daring leaders" – they show up, they create safe places for learners to be brave, learn, and grow, Brown opines. When I heard Brown say this, I kept thinking about the teachers I'd worked with in Afghanistan – intelligent, informed, and eager to learn and change how they taught. But they were isolated with limited connections or opportunities to connect with those outside their country. They listening intently to my stories of TESOL work and teachers elsewhere who, like them, were working hard to help their students learn, wanting to be leaders. TESOL professionals are great leaders – they allow themselves vulnerability, they are smart communicators, they operate in cultures of information sharing, and they put their students' needs before their own. As we move through our TESOL careers, we need to better and more intentionally draw on our developing leadership skills.

The work of Anne Loehr, regularly updated on her website at www.AnneLoehr.com as well as Emerson in *The Washington Post*, February 25, 2009, shows how important it is for leaders and organizations to address the new challenges brought on by first-in-history workplace environments in the United States where four generations might share the same tasks. These issues will be different for those in other workplace settings, countries, and cultures.

TESOL professionals have more job satisfaction and perform better too when they feel empowered to make changes. TESOL leaders resemble corporate leaders in that respect. In a recent article published in an online blog, major representatives of major corporations reflect on this fact "When the workforce feels customers are dissatisfied, and they can't do anything about it because they don't have the discretion to solve [problems], you get a reinforcing cycle of very low morale and frustrated people," he said. "The employees feel like they're bearing the brunt of the customer service problems and can't do anything about them" (Relihan, 2019). Reminiscent of conversations I have had with colleagues and former students and those you may well have had too, TESOL professionals frequently lack opportunities and the power to make changes in their programs. At all stages of career path development, top-down management that ignores excellence in TESOL, ESL, or EFL teaching staff creates burnout and dissatisfaction (and ultimately job resignations).

We need to know more about how TESOLers become leaders, focusing less on telling them how to do it and what to do. TESOL leadership isn't a club, it's a lifestyle that includes work that is useful to others and satisfying for oneself. What are the components of TESOL leadership at the five stages of career path development identified here? How does leadership evolve in different program types and cultural contexts internationally? There is much work to do to help us to better understand TESOL leadership throughout our careers.

References

Adoniou, M. (2019). [presentation handout] TESOL 2019 Conference, Chicago IL.

Amzat, I. H., & Valdez, N. P. (Eds.). (2017). *Teacher empowerment and practices: perspectives across borders*. Singapore: Springer Singapore.

Brown, B. (2010, June). The power of vulnerability [video file]. Retrieved from https://www.ted.com/talks/brene_brown_on_vulnerability?language=en

Emerson, B. (2009). A manager's guide to coaching – simple and effective ways to get the best out of your employees. *Development and Learning in Organizations: An International Journal*, (23), 3, https://doi.org/10.1108/dlo.2009.08123cae.001

Harrison, C. H., & Killion, J. (2007). Ten roles for teacher leaders. *Educational Leadership, 65*(1). Retrieved from http://www.ascd.org/publications/educational-leadership/sept07/vol65/num01/Ten-Roles-for-Teacher-Leaders.aspx

Loucks-Horsley Susan. (1996). The design of templates as tools for formative evaluation. *Special Issue: A User's Guide to Program Templates: A New Tool for Evaluating Program Content, 1996*(72), 5–24.

Summit on the future of the TESOL profession, Athens Greece. (2017, February 10, 11). Retrieved from https://www.tesol.org/summit-2017

68 Leadership

Talmage, C., Knopf, R. C. (2017). Rethinking diversity, inclusion, and inclusiveness: The quest to better understand indicators of community enrichment and well-being. In P. Kraeger., S. Cloutier., & C. Talmage (Eds) *New dimensions in community well-being. Community quality-of-life and well-being.* Cham: Springer.

Tannacito, D. (2013). What, me? An administrator? *English language teachers as program administrators.* Alexandria, VA: TESOL Publications.

TESOL Leadership (n.d.). TESOL leadership certificate program. Retrieved from https://sites.tesol.org/MemberPortal/Events/2018/PL18_LDCP/TESOL-Event-Detail?EventKey=PL18_LDCP

What is Teacher Leadership? (n.d.). Retrieved from http://www.ascd.org/publications/books/105048/chapters/What-Is-Teacher-Leadership%C2%A2.aspx

7

LIFE BALANCE

Overview

For many of us, it doesn't take a move to a new country to create a sense of life imbalance. Personal changes, even happy ones, can create imbalance: a new baby, marriage, separation, or divorce, taking an extra job to make ends meet, the loss of a family member to death or disease, or a personal illness or injury. While some of these are "good news," the fact that a big change in one's personal life has occurred can lead to a sense of imbalance.

In a recent public radio broadcast, a political leader in the United States said that "teachers are losers" (Karnitz, 2019). He said that students shouldn't do what their teachers tell them to do because teachers are incompetent. While such messages are distortions and exaggerations of the truth (there are, in my opinion, very few teachers who are losers), they have a significant impact on teachers when such messages come to us on a daily diet. Nowadays, teachers worldwide get too many of these negative messages. In the United States, for example, ESL (English as a Second Language) teachers in particular deal with the negative attitudes and sometimes outright hostility from political leaders. This, combined with the ever-present messages of fear and hate toward immigrants and minorities, who together represent many of our students, creates a difficult environment for teachers nowadays. Such comments as the one described above weigh heavily on TESOL (Teachers of English to Speakers of Other Languages) professionals who hear it every day. And professional performance and morale are low in these times.

Professional life changes can be equally as upsetting for our sense of balance: a new title or job responsibility, a new boss, a conflict with a colleague, a

70 Life Balance

negative evaluation, a new software system for entering data, failed efforts with a particularly difficult class, and a myriad of other changes on the job. No matter what job we have or where we are working, life is about making things work. No matter how much we weigh or how complex our job responsibilities are, we must consider what makes us happy – on the job and on off hours. Body, mind, and soul – those are what make us complex, creative, productive, and fully human. In this chapter, I will present an exploration on TESOL career path and factors of life balance that are at play as we move along.

Saying no is hard for teachers; and so, we often just say yes to everything. We are culturally engrained to say yes; we often fail at setting boundaries, and institutional cultures sometimes take advantage of us. In extreme cases, workplaces are toxic and then we face a decision of whether or not to resign from our jobs – stay and be abused or leave and be unemployed. These are obviously two not-good situations in which to find oneself. But too often we do find ourselves in these lose-lose positions. Ingersoll, Merrill, and Stuckey (2014) found that after five years, 40–50% of teachers left the profession. And our language – to ourselves and to our students as well – reflects these facts: "You cannot; you need to; you may not ..." We need to learn to set boundaries and create better balance in our personal and professional priorities and boundaries.

How do TESOLers at various stages of their careers take care of themselves? How do we cope with the challenges of today's world without anger, discouragement, and hate? And finally, how can we avoid "the victim syndrome" – feeling that everyone and everything is against us?

In Chapter 5, we saw how getting fired is a big deal. How to get up the next morning? How to move on with our careers? In Chapter 8, we will be analyzing career path milestones – events that occur in our lives that have great impact on our professional careers. In other chapters, I try to describe extraordinary successes in various aspects of one's career. How to use successes to move forward? Throughout our careers, what makes it possible for us to learn, grow, and change and at the same time maintain a sense of equilibrium and balance? In this chapter, I will address the final aspect of TESOL career path development: life balance.

In their extensive research on the issues in work-life balance, published in *Employee Relations*, Eikhof, Warhurst, and Haunschild (2007) conclude that new definitions are needed to address better explanations from those forwarded in the past for what life balance is for the future. In this chapter, I will make a small step toward that new definition. According to a recent report in a commercially available magazine called *Better Health* (2012), the following is a list of sources of and responses to job-related stress: "Long hours, heavy workload, job insecurity and conflicts with co-workers or bosses. Symptoms include a drop in work performance, depression, anxiety and sleeping difficulties. It is important for employers to recognise work-related stress as a significant health and safety issue."

Story

For the first time in her professional life, 35-year-old assistant professor, Jackie, a Canadian, moved to a new country to take a teaching job in a religious academic institution. She was teaching undergraduate courses in second language acquisition and English language teaching methods to majors in an "English Pedagogy" program with service on the Curriculum Committee, and making presentations on English teaching and use in other university departments. While new colleagues and friends were helpful to her in adjusting to her new life, there were many adjustments for her that were difficult: restrictions on her movements (no walking alone outside), her appearance (head cover required at all times except inside her own home), her interactions with men (she was advised to avoid long meetings with any male colleagues or others at work and to avoid inviting men to visit her at home), and absence of other familiar routines seemed overwhelming. Extreme strain on her body, mind, and soul came fast in the first few months of her stay. Her morning jog – something she'd done every day for the past ten years – was no longer possible; the big load of learning her new job, teaching classes, and attending meetings made it impossible to take a class or otherwise engage in any new learning opportunities; and her lifelong religious community offered neither services nor gatherings in her new city. Jackie noticed signs of ill-health, head and body aches, lethargy, and even anger with others. Knowing that there are phases of adjustment and social distance progresses through stages, she tried to be patient, awaiting the day she would feel less stressed and return to her usual sense of balance and productivity. Jackie's life had become unbalanced.

Life balance allows us the opportunity and responsibility for self-care for our whole selves: body, mind, and soul. As professionals in the 21st century, we need life balance, which I present here, as the final component of an analysis of career path development in TESOL. Most research separates work from life. Here, I see work as a part of life and efforts to balance one's life to include efforts to manage one's work life as a part of overall life balance.

Some have confused life balance with emotional intelligence. Life balance is not emotional intelligence. Emotional intelligence is the ability to use emotional behavior cues to monitor, identify, and understand oneself or others. Life balance is less a skill and more how we experience our lives focusing on the three life balance components: body, mind, and soul. And while most people who engage in a variety of efforts to balance their lives find benefit in all three, the following analysis is designed to "take apart" life balance. The process of taking it apart will provide opportunities for interested readers to develop insights and perhaps effective tools for addressing their own career path development and self-care.

I will then put it back together again, Humpty Dumpty style, in order to set the groundwork for the final section of this chapter on some questions for

72 Life Balance

further investigation for those who may be seeking to do research on the effects of life balance on TESOL career path development.

Balance/Imbalance

Day to day, TESOLers face a variety of threats to balance in their lives. I make no claim to address all of those; but here is a list of those that have come to me through the stories of colleagues, former students, and former colleagues. I present here the top four threats to life balance for TESOLers in my circle, a group of 50 teachers at all stages of career path development and working in 12 countries worldwide. Those five threats are bad boss, stress and too long work hours, lack of appreciation, and family demands.

Bad boss: There is neither a country nor any English program where bosses don't exist. In the stories of over 50 TESOLers (at all stages of their careers), "bad boss" was listed in the vast majority of the stories as the biggest threat to life and work balance. Leaders in the workplace, referred to here as "good bosses," help teachers to teach effectively, engage in valuable research projects, and provide service – to the profession and to the community.

In the same survey, teachers said that by contrast, a "bad boss" has the opposite effect; and for those in my informal study, a bad boss can be the deal breaker for a teacher in a job where they might be otherwise satisfied.

A good boss (individuals whose job it is to manage and/or lead) create an environment of trust. Trust is established and sustained when leaders support excellence, create and lead teams, and support innovation and change in line with updates in practice, and a respectful work context. A bad boss creates an environment of mistrust, little or no support of excellence, resistance to innovation and change, and disrespectful behavior in the workplace.

Many teachers leave their jobs because of a bad boss. And while people become bosses through a myriad of fascinating and sometimes circuitous routes, not all bosses belong in their jobs; and some are smart to step down from their positions before they harm themselves or those who work for them. There is nothing better to support healthy career path development in TESOL than an excellent boss. Another book might address them.

Work-related stress: Some sources indicate that teachers suffer more stress than any other types of workers. Working intensively over a shorter period of time with students who may face extreme life struggles can be extremely stressful, leading to physical, mental, and spiritual crises for teachers. Stressed out TESOL professionals deal every day with the realities of students who may have learning disabilities, have endured trauma (refugees and asylum seekers of all ages take English classes in the United States and elsewhere worldwide), or have emotional problems. ESL teachers frequently deal with the challenges of low budgets, large classes, and poor working conditions. In some schools, ESL is considered as a second-class program for students who are often disenfranchised or marginalized. Teachers in these programs face extreme stress. Teachers' life balance is threatened by these work-related stressful issues.

Too long work hours: As a helping profession, teaching can occupy longer than 40 hours a week of work. Few teachers work as little as 40 hours per week. However, overworking can lead to imbalance. And with it, many teachers get tired and angry – blaming their boss or someone else for their struggles. A state of teacher anger can be our own worst enemy, creating a context for a spiral down into depression or worse. Teachers must advocate for themselves, avoiding falling into a spiral in to victimhood and blaming others for their lot. By learning early in their careers about how to advocate on their own behalf, teachers are better prepared to deal with imbalance at work than they might have been without advocacy training early in their careers.

Unappreciated work: The extent to which one's work is appreciated will impact a sense of balance. Teachers who are appreciated have a better sense of balance in their work lives. Here, appreciation is defined as the act of acknowledging another's good qualities, strengths, and/or abilities. In her research on teacher morale, Blackburn (2015) interviewed teachers in four schools. The results are compelling and show that the institutional context makes a difference in teacher morale. And the one feature that subjects in her study identified as essential to morale was appreciation. The one school, where appreciation was intentional, frequent, and carefully attended to by the boss and encouraged throughout the staff, had high levels of job satisfaction and teacher retention.

Family demands: Family commitments have an impact on life balance. When families face unexpected problems, it's more difficult for a teacher to be able to attend to work tasks and to have a general sense of balance and well-being. Throughout our careers in TESOL, we experience a wide range of family responsibilities that influence the extent to which we are able to manage life balance. TESOL professionals, like everyone, make choices about employment opportunities. And jobs may take us far from our parents and older siblings. Depending on local customs and norms, there is social pressure to address family issues first, before tending to professional responsibilities. How do TESOLers worldwide balance work and family obligations? With almost no research on the role of family obligations in professional career path development, the time is ripe for addressing this important factor.

How do family obligations affect preservice teachers (graduate students) compared to, for example, veteran teachers? How and to what extent do bosses, language teacher associations, and others support teachers with family issues?

In order to research the role of life balance in TESOL career path development, we first must address life balance. And based on an assumption (and anecdotal evidence) of its importance to TESOL career path development, I will present a definition of life balance: Life balance means the comfortable

74 Life Balance

interconnection among these three components – body, mind, and soul. By addressing all three, we can hope for more balance in our professional lives at all stages of our career paths.

Body: Taking care of our physical bodies is part of our professional responsibility.

How do TESOL professionals take care of their physical bodies? Regular physical exercise is the answer. Are we, individually, engaged in programs of regular physical exercise? How do we address self-care of our bodies at different stages of our careers? Do groups of teachers differ from others based on where they live, whom they teach, and what phase they are on their career paths?

Mind: Engaging in activities that force us to actively use our cognitive skills, knowledge, and problem-solving skills is an essential practice for every TESOL professional. How and to what extent are we different from other professional groups in terms of ways in which we engage in keeping our minds healthy and active?

Soul: Spiritual health is essential to overall professional development. How and to what extent do TESOL professionals find ways to engage their souls as they move from one stage to the next of their TESOL careers.

While most TESOL professionals are women and our comments here generally focus on them, it is of course the case that men in our field also benefit from self-care. A recent search on a major Internet site provides a look at the tens of books on the topic of self-care. These books include more or less documented effective ways in which those in a variety of fields address burnout and other job-related stress. Both online and face-to-face courses offer opportunities for self-care – mindfulness-based stress reduction, yoga, meditation, physical exercise programs, and pharmaceutical products, to name several. There is new interest in the topic of balancing one's life! And for those who may be wary of the realities of burnout or may doubt its power and impact, the World Health Organization (WHO) has just identified burnout as an official medical diagnosis. No longer relegated to those among us who've been called "weak" or "unbalanced," burnouts are now officially among those recognized as having a medical condition (Prior, 2019).

When we feel stuck with imbalance, it can be helpful to let go of our resistance to the change that wants to come forth. A recent article in *The Atlantic Magazine* outlines very recent research on mindfulness for teachers and students. In addition to describing the ways in which mindfulness can improve students' attention and emotional regulation, the author, Lauren Cassani Davis, interviewed Gonzalez and Greenburg, two psychologists leading these studies, both of whom describe the even greater impact of mindfulness on teacher education.

Gonzalez ultimately thinks that mindfulness may go furthest if applied to teacher education as a way to help prevent burnout – a major issue, gen that 20 percent of teachers in high-poverty schools leave within their first year. Greenberg agrees. Of the ongoing research projects he and his colleagues are involved in is the

Cultivating Awareness and Resilience in Education (CARE) program, funded by the United States Department of Education. This study focuses on the well-being of the teacher and instructs teachers on emotional awareness, techniques for emotional regulation, and ways to apply these skills to teaching. Greenburg and others suspect that mindfulness specifically tailored to teachers and their struggles – stress and time management for example – and incorporated into their initial training might do as much or more to improve classroom performance than trying to teach children directly. In its annual surveys, Mindful Schools has found that a majority of the teachers it has trained experienced lower stress, more connection with students, and higher job satisfaction (Davis, 2015). There are opponents to mindfulness as well; and in the same article, Davis describes the fact that the numbers of those who reject mindfulness practices in schools are decreasing, "… belief-based critiques are becoming less common."

Most of us can relate to one or more of the four areas of imbalance reported by TESOL professionals interviewed for this book. Who among us has not experienced those? I encourage us all to consider mindfulness as a part of addressing the rewards and milestones as well as the challenges and sometimes unpleasant realities of today's TESOL world.

Wherever we are on our career paths in the global world of TESOL, we can benefit from mindfulness in addressing work-related challenges. And in the good times, too, we do well to be mindful as well – What joys do we know in our work lives? What might have transpired at work – what someone said, what we overheard, or what we ourselves might have done – that raised our mood, that elated us, or that encouraged us? Mindfulness can be helpful throughout our careers in TESOL – offering opportunities to explore ways in which this career choice has had an impact on our lives. In Chapter 6, I presented "Rewards and Challenges" in career path development. Mindfully writing those down and reflecting on our work lives can be helpful to us all, regardless of where we are on our TESOL career path.

Mindfulness can help us find out if there is something we are doing or not doing that is keeping us stuck. Sometimes, the situation is out of our control and we need to look within to find patience required to wait with equanimity until things move forward again. Many times, we can find the source of our stagnation in our own hearts and minds. Sometimes we are clinging to old ideas about reality and we need to make adjustments that will bring us back in tune with life so we can flow again. Sometimes, fear of change is what's keeping us stuck and we can resolve to find ways of facing that fear. You can find it inside or you can find it in the words of a trusted, good friend. What do you notice that isn't obvious to me? Let go of resistance to what you hear. Fear sometimes blocks our ability to hear. What you need is what you know best. Be kind to yourself. Then you can figure things out. Meditation, prayer, and yoga can be helpful ways of doing all this.

76 Life Balance

In the work–life balance debate, overwork is perceived as the problem. Nevertheless, beyond working time and the provision of flexible working practices to enable child care, there is little in the debate about the need to change work per se. The debate also narrowly perceives "life," equating it with women's care work, hence the emphasis again of family-friendly policies. We know that sources of imbalance and burnout are both inside the workplace and outside. At work, we deal with weak and strong supervisors, supportive colleagues and those who want to do us harm, students who work with, us and those who fight us every step of the way – those who want to learn and make our days bright and there are also those who resist engaging in the learning experience and want to engage in power dynamics and other distractions from learning.

Note: What's here is based on a US-based analysis; so, as is always the case, I encourage colleagues worldwide in non-US settings, to address these issues for their own professional contexts. While there may well be overlaps (between what readers see here and what goes on in their professional settings), it is likely that results will differ for TESOLers elsewhere. And since there are so many teachers elsewhere, it is timely and fitting to encourage further research elsewhere, particularly among those non-native English-speaking teachers' programs and settings.

Recommendations

What follows is a list of general recommendations for those TESOL colleagues – present and future – seeking ways to improve their lives through more balance. The list is divided into three parts, as previously described above, body, mind, and soul. Where research exists to support the suggestions provided, the source is provided. In other cases, the recommendation is based only on anecdotal evidence.

Regular self-assessment can be a good way to start thinking about your own TESOL life balance. Writing it down can be a healthy step in moving ahead on your TESOL career path. What is the state of your body? Mind? Soul? What happened in your work life – now or at some time in the past – that might have led you to imbalance? How can you limit the chances of its happening again? What can you do to bring balance to your work life? And what can you stop doing that might be contributing to imbalance? These are a few starter questions for those who may be interested in addressing life balance as a part of TESOL career path development (Table 7.1).

Here, I've reviewed a number of ways to "re-balance" one's life as we move through our TESOL careers. In closing and because I promised, here I offer the following, an initial list of ongoing issues and some initial responses to those seeking additional help at various stages of their careers. These inquiries have come to me from former students, mentees, and colleagues worldwide following

Life Balance **77**

TABLE 7.1 Some strategies for English language teachers' life balance at five career stages

TESOL career path stage	Body	Mind	Soul
Preservice	Healthy eating – when you're living as a graduate student, there's a tendency to eat fast and poorly – do neither!	Reflecting frequently on the new knowledge and skills one is acquiring quickly	Practicing emotional resilience activities for life: optimism, facing fears, morality, and spirituality
Novice	Physical exercise, designed to build strength, endurance, and flexibility	Avoid tendency to do it all. Take an art class – get away from the workplace on time	Take a pause now and then – for example – meditation, hiking
Mid-career/ career switcher	Avoid physical overdoing (it's easy to think you can do anything you think you can do!)	Identify a new work-related tool (electronic, tech, other) and buy it!	Try something new – a new way to practice your spiritual beliefs, a new spiritual practice
Veteran	Find a physical exercise program that you like and exercise every day; change the program now and then (after a few months)	Identify a part of the world about which you want to learn more; learn the language! Find a pen friend there and communicate online	Make a new friend and reconnect with an old friend; socialize! Find a role model and consider that person's spiritual habits. *Note:* Even a bad role model can be a good teacher! Take a trip
Semiretired	Yoga – it helps with stress and it's great for maintaining physical flexibility	Improve flexibility of thinking – try to see things in a wide lens and don't get stuck in a narrow-minded way of doing things	Find meaning in what you do; activities that give you joy, a sense of contribution, and achievement are the ones to do; skip the others!

Note: While strategies are identified here with one stage on your TESOL career path, one can use many of the strategies at other phases as well. The strategies have been recommended by those who have tried them; they are examples, not a definitive list.

the completion of the first draft of this chapter, and so, I have added them. Apologies in advance for the randomness of the contents of this list, a reflection more of the limited research already done. In many cases, the research occupies a rich field of study in other professions and disciplines; and in other cases, there is simply nothing available to draw on and so anecdotal evidence is offered. More

78 Life Balance

research will lead to fewer anecdotal items and more data- and research-driven recommendations and trends.

1. How to utilize self-assessments?
2. What to do with a bad workplace evaluation?
3. How to quit your job?
    Knowing when a job is a bad match for you and how to leave a job as a novice teacher takes knowledge, skills, and strategies that differ from other groups. Mid-career and career switchers face specific challenges when they make the choice to leave a job in TESOL.
4. How to kick-start your career?
5. Some advice for older teachers?

The value of older workers and the roles of semiretirees in the workplace has been described in Yeatts, Folts, and Knapp (2000). While concerns about older workers manifest in different ways, this research identifies three major challenges for older teachers: lack of compensation and benefits, a sense of belonging, and diversity and inclusion. This challenge was best described in an article in Forbes Magazine (2017).

Yeatts et al. (2000) identify the problem for older workers in their research on how older workers adapt to change:

> Our review of the literature shows that there are a variety of factors at the individual, organizational, and environmental levels that affect an older worker's ability and choice to adjust to workplace changes. These factors include, for example, training throughout an individual's career, personnel policies affecting older workers, and age discrimination. (p. 562)

TESOLers worldwide are graying. While reliable data on age of members is unavailable, it has been repeatedly said that more than half of the members of TESOL International Association count themselves as 50 years of age or more. What can TESOL and ESL programs and professional associations do to find ways to retrain, advocate for, and utilize the mature values and experience of our older colleagues? Some semiretirees do volunteer projects with social justice groups; others find part-time work in local schools, colleges, and universities; others do selected consulting and lecturing projects worldwide. How can (and to what extent should we) mine the knowledge, skills, and experience of older TESOL professionals?

As outlined here, this chapter is an effort to identify and differentiate life balance as a part of TESOL career path development. What follows is a description of some items to include in addressing that critical part of our whole lives. Life balance is a part of who we are (identity) and what we do (teaching, research,

Life Balance **79**

and service) that is as essential as knowledge and skills in TESOL but too often overlooked.

Consider these tips in balancing your life:

> Have you had a career milestone – a major life event – marriage, divorce, new job, or promotion? Have you experienced heartbreak – professional or personal?

1. *Self-assessment:* Keep notes, all year, on your job performance and efforts. Know that without these notes, you will forget or run victim to the memories and/or records of others when facing a job evaluation or when you seek a new job or perhaps some other context in which you want to succinctly describe your achievements.

   In her recent article in *The Washington Post*, Johanns (2018, December 30) provides some ideas on self-assessment that have been useful to TESOLers: In addition to keeping notes (#1 above), Johanns offers these reminders: understand the purpose of a self-assessment. In some TESOL contexts, self-assessment is the only record of our contributions at work; in other contexts, there are numerous assessments. Know how your self-assessment is to be used. Take it seriously and try not to be afraid to provide details on what you do well. Make sure to describe intentions in areas of weakness. Being honest about your performance is important; but it doesn't mean addressing only strengths; and it doesn't mean listing all weaknesses. Hold yourself accountable by including evidence in notes – statistical and brief narrative evidence will help support claims on your efforts to address weaknesses. Stay forward-focused – too often, we fixate on evaluations, particularly the bad ones; and in so doing, we tend to focus more on the past than the future, a sure block to improvement. And finally, prioritize your professional growth by avoiding a tendency to sideline or put our own professional developmental needs second or third to other priorities. Our professional development is our own responsibility. We should embrace opportunities to grow through self-assessment.

2. *The factors that influence life balance change as we move through our careers in TESOL:* In his recent book, *Putting Teachers First: How To Inspire, Motivate and Connect with Your Staff,* Johnson (2019) recently identifies nine topics that TESOLers at all stages of their career paths might want to consider: teacher satisfaction, motivation to succeed, being a part of a culture of appreciation, learn to become selfless leaders, remember their purpose, develop emotional intelligence, communicate and connect effectively, build teams that are cohesive, and functional and celebrate successes. Here, I invite readers to consider this list as a starting point for balancing our TESOL lives.

80 Life Balance

3. *Coping with imbalance demands a great deal of energy and TESOLers can learn from the research and recommendations offered in a variety of life balance research and/or self-help columns:* Research supports these: the value of rituals with family, friends, and colleagues; mindful breathing; and strategies such as "stop-drop-relax:" when the heat's on, use one of these strategies or others to help regain balance. In some cases, counseling and coaching professionals can support efforts to achieve better life balance. And finally, when depression and burnout are extreme, various treatments are available. Here's a list of some of those: inhalants like esketamine, acupuncture treatments, yoga and Pilates, counseling, and antidepressant drug treatment. Job burnout should never be ignored. Symptoms include sleep loss, appetite loss, feelings of worthlessness, and signs of poor performance. If you're burned out, get help. Don't wait for others to do it for you. Coping means take care of ourselves.

Like teachers everywhere, TESOLers must take initiative to look after themselves in ways that many of us have failed to do. As has been addressed elsewhere in this book, taking care of ourselves means our students have daily models that show them how to take care of themselves too. A well-cared teacher – one who values himself/herself – will provide a model for students to do the same. What follows here is a final recommendation – on addressing life balance by caring for our bodies, minds, and souls. Our professional success demands that we do this. Note: We have limits on what we can comfortably manage – emotional limits and time limits on what we can do. Try to view those as a benefit – offering us opportunities to focus and set priorities we want to address.

Body: Get prepared: know what a normal blood pressure is, healthy waist/height ratio, update insurance, go to the dentist (and floss!), check the mirror: eyes, eyelids, lips, teeth, tongue, and face; get enough sleep (but not too much), take a selfie and if you see something unusual, show it to your doctor; engage in regular physical activity; check your grip, flexibility, and ability to get up from seated position on the floor (no hands!); and join a sports team and do squats and lunges. Practice balance exercises and eat well (or at least a little better) – fiber, fruits, and vegetables; nuts and seeds; cut out meat and make time for tea and coffee breaks with friends. Get outside – take a walk, even for five minutes (research shows that it works to take an outdoor break).

Mind: Throw a party, book a tour (it doesn't have to be the big, expensive time) – a local winery tour, a museum trip; do occasional self-assessments on your ability to manage stress, finances, engagement. Learn a new language, to play a new sport or be a tutor or mentor for someone who needs one. The best advice I have ever given anyone at any career stage: Don't cling to a dying professional role or job. Find a new one. And finally, hang out sometimes with people who are a different age from you. While like-minded folks who are also similar in age are great, research shows it's good for the mind, body, and soul to mix it up with those different from ourselves. As ESL teachers, our students are a great resource to help us.

Soul: Get out of negative relationships, both face-to-face and social media, thank your spouse and close friends; use your smart phone but not too much (and not while driving). Our roles and identity change throughout our careers. While retaining one's values, faith, and principles, we can also be open to change.

At the TESOL International Association 2017 Summit (where forward planning for TESOL worldwide was the agenda), four themes emerged: Futurology, English and multilingualism, Reimagining English competence, and the Profession as change agent. How do we make changes? How do we resist change? How can the profession function to help teachers change? And how can TESOL International Association affect change in our profession? Individual teachers ("micro level") can inspire change; systems (here, Chapter 5 on Organizational Development) are the "meso" level, the contexts in which teachers work; and finally, society is the wider ranging and heavily influential "macro" level of change. How do these three levels function; how can we utilize these descriptions to create research projects and to investigate ways in which they work individually (and/or collaboratively, together) to help teachers become better advocates for themselves and their programs and their students, to have audiences and be listened to in policy setting meetings, and to be prepared to deal with the familiar and most certainly new challenges ahead? Indeed, advocacy is an essential component in TESOL career path development. It's part of having a balanced life and I address it in more depth in Chapter 10.

I close this chapter on life balance for TESOLers throughout their careers with the most fitting description I could find of the essence of TESOL life balance for career path development in the words of Nepal English Language Teachers Association President, Meera Shrestha, at the TESOL Summit in 2017: "We are all in this together." And to that I would add, "throughout our careers!" We balance ourselves alongside our stakeholders in TESOL.

References

Better Health Channel. (2012). Work-related stress. Retrieved from https://www.betterhealth.vic.gov.au/health/healthyliving/work-related-stress

Blackburn, J. (2015). *An evaluation of teacher morale in four elementary schools: The difference a school makes* (Dissertation). Retrieved from https://digitalcommons.nl.edu/diss/118/

Davis, L. C. (2015, August 31). When mindfulness meets the classroom. *The Atlantic Magazine.* Retrieved from https://www.theatlantic.com/education/archive/2015/08/mindfulness-education-schools-meditation/402469/

Eikhof, D. R., Warhurst, C., & Haunschild, A. (2007). Introduction: What work? What life? What balance? Critical reflections on the work-life balance debate. *Employee Relations, 29*(4), 325–339.

82 Life Balance

Ingersoll, R., Merrill, L., & Stuckey, D. (2014). Seven trends: The transformation of the teaching force. *CPRE Research Reports*. Retrieved from https://repository.upenn.edu/cpre_researchreports/79 and http://www.cpre.org/sites/default/files/workingpapers/1506_7trendsapril2014.pdf

Johanns, K. (2018, December 30). How successful people write their self-reviews. *The Washington Post*. Retrieved from https://www.pressreader.com/usa/the-washington-post.../20181230/283085595307359

Johnson, B. (2019). *Putting teachers first: How to inspire, motivate and connect with your staff*. New York: Routledge Taylor & Francis.

Karnitz, K. (2019, February 14). Opinion: Teachers aren't losers. Retrieved from https://www.pbs.org/newshour/education/opinion-teachers-arent-losers-theyre-lifesavers

Prior, R. (2019, May 27). Burnout is an official medical diagnosis, World Health Organization says. Retrieved from https://www.cnn.com/2019/05/27/health/who-burnout-disease-trnd/index.html?no-st=1559226612

Shrestha, M. (2017). *Closing Remarks*. Paper presented at the 2017 TESOL Summit, Athens, Greece.

Yeatts, D., Folts, E., & Knapp, J. (2000). Older workers adaptation to a changing workplace: Employment issues for the 21st century. *Educational Gerontology, 26*(6), 565–582. https://doi.org/10.1080/03601270050133900

8

REWARDS AND MILESTONES

Rewards

Rewards are both formal and informal professional recognition of our hard work and achievements. Formal rewards are those bestowed upon us by our workplace and supervisors, our professional associations: TESOL (Teaching English to Speakers of Other Languages) Teacher of the Year, … A pay raise is a formal reward and we have too few of those in most TESOL settings! Informal rewards come from our personal networks – families, friends, colleagues, former students, and mentees. Formal and informal rewards alike feed our sense of purpose, our motivation, and yes, our egos too. Without rewards, we simply do not move forward in our careers. In his recent book, *Putting Teachers First*, containing useful descriptions for helping teachers of all specializations to support themselves and to be supported by others, Johnson (2019) devotes an entire chapter to "Celebrating Successes." Johnson goes so far as to provide readers with a list of "Keys to effective recognition and praise" (pp. 128–131).

Formal and informal expressions of appreciation and recognition make it possible to endure the bad times (inevitable in human experience); and, as is the case for all professionals, we need those to have successful careers in TESOL. When we face milestones in our careers, we rely on our rewards – formal and informal – to help us navigate them.

Elton (2009), in his research on appreciation for performance at work (including data from both employers and employees), identifies some surprising statistics: 79% of employees who quit cite lack of appreciation as the cause; in addition, two of the top four responses to "what do you really want from your job?" were (1) recognition and (2) better relationships with managers (pp. 3–9).

84 Rewards and Milestones

Appreciation is important for teachers; and TESOLers often report a sense of not being appreciated by others. But we are professionals and so we rarely complain about it publicly. Within the safety and trust of our families and close colleagues, many of us have complained and most of us have heard complaints from others. There are times in our professional lives when burnout looms close and we seek the comfort of friends and family members and other good listeners in darker times. Working with non-native English-speaking students often means that we are identified by supervisors and other administrators and sometimes even peers in other academic disciplines as being lower, lesser, and/or more dispensable. It's easy to feel unhappy, dissatisfied, and underappreciated in those work environments. Identifying rewards and milestones can be a first step in addressing those negative feelings. Beyond our "inner circles," there is the possibility of more support for and appreciation of our professional efforts.

I wrote in Chapter 5 about the importance of organizations in TESOL career path development. When we work in a place where there is a team of professional colleagues who appreciate each other and are appreciated by managers, supervisors, and administrators, we can express our passion for our teaching, research, and service activities and we can grow in our sense of professional identities. With a sense of trust in our colleagues and supervisors, a commitment to the progress of ourselves as members of teams and with opportunities for both giving and receiving (even small) expressions of appreciation for our efforts – these are what create milestones. The struggles are inevitable; but the rewards are what drive us to be better and to do better. And we have known for decades that teachers with higher morale are more productive (Kahn & Katz, 1952). Professional associations do some to create a sense of appreciation of "work well done" with awards for exemplary professional activities: Teacher of the Year and various annual recognitions at conventions of a handful of teachers. More efforts are needed on the part of professional associations to recognize and appreciate larger numbers of members for excellence in teaching, research, and service. In Chapter 9, I have provided some suggested steps for workplace and professional associations' leadership to acknowledge excellence and to help all teachers to identify and pursue their own sense of being appreciated and to pursue their professional development goals.

We all have stories of very dedicated English language teachers. Whether it was an extraordinary lesson where students engaged enthusiastically with learning to use a new grammar rule or a hug or help with a visa application, social media offers daily reminders of teachers who do big things for students. These teachers inspire their students. But they also inspire their colleagues. And indeed, many inspire the whole world of English language learners!

Rewards are great, right? It's gratifying and helpful to be appreciated, to be recognized, and to put a plaque or certificate on a wall and have others see it and admire our professional achievements and efforts. It is my sincere wish for all TESOLers to know rewards of all kinds and frequently. Rewards are positive and they sometimes even change the way we do things, moving us forward along our career paths. In the next section, I'll address another source of our progress along our TESOL career paths — milestones are what really push us forward. Sometimes, milestones are also rewards. But in other cases, milestones aren't rewards at all.

Milestones

Milestones are those events in our careers during which we make a significant change; sometimes, as is the case for rewards, milestones move us to a new professional title; others come in the form of personal events (marriage or the birth of child). In ancient times, a stone was set up beside a road to mark the distance in miles to a particular place. TESOL milestones mark events and/or periods of transition in our careers. Sometimes, those milestones are rewards; and sometimes (as we saw in the story in Chapter 7 about M and her firing) those feel like boulders that crash down on our heads! In all cases, milestones help us move forward along our TESOL career paths.

So, in addition to rewards, some have described professional challenges — crises, disasters, and grief as they move through their careers. Sometimes even sad times can be milestones — job loss, health issues, or the loss of a family member: a parent dies, or divorce, or separation from spouse or partner. TESOLers are no different from other international professionals in that we face struggles — sometimes very hard ones — caused by personal catastrophes, political turmoil, natural disasters, and professional crises. Milestones can come to us as good things — a promotion at our current job, a new job in a new institution in our own countries, or even a job in a foreign country. Many TESOL are often what might be described as "geographically mobile" — seeking opportunities to find new professional challenges and travel. Many of us are also professionally motivated to find new challenges. With these goals, TESOLers have opportunities for adventure with new opportunities for professional growth that require a significant physical move to another part of one country or, as often, to a foreign country.

Based on my own experience and that reported by many others in our field, TESOLers have an uncanny skill to turn some struggles into milestones. And while not all struggles are milestones, what at the time might appear to be a significantly painful experience is often seen later to have been a milestone: what might seem to have been a bad experience at the time might later be seen as a critical turning point in one's career. Many of us have had such experiences — we thought we had a great job and then one day, a new supervisor replaces our old, wonderful one. And what were previously cheerful, fulfilling work days become a drudgery. By the same token, a terrible boss goes away and a wonderful one comes in to our lives. What we know today might change tomorrow. And the forces of workplace change are many for TESOLers.

86 Rewards and Milestones

What are some significant rewards and milestones in your career? In several workshops in a half-dozen countries, I have asked participants this question. Answers are profoundly diverse and here I will relay a few of those. Notice as you read these how each has an element of "reward" and "milestone." Notice, too, the fact that each contains elements of life balance: body, mind, or soul. Not all are positive, not all are negative experiences. All weigh in the memories of those who've experienced these and the individuals who've kindly agreed to allow me to use these examples of TESOL career path milestones will be glad to fill in the details for you. I hope to show here how rewards and milestones can and do shape our TESOL career paths.

Story 1: Julie and The Cops

Julie had graduated two years earlier with a Master's degree in TESOL from a strong and internationally recognized university. Upon graduation, the same university hired Julie to work in their Intensive English Program, where she was familiar with the program culture, the students, and the work to be done. A year later, she'd had it – "I'm so sick of this place! Same thing, every day!" she complained to me on a phone call she'd scheduled to address what she called "a professional turning point." After an hour's chat, we determined that Julie needed to apply for new jobs. Eight months later, she was on a plane to Indonesia. The next years would bring, what I and everyone who knew her, extraordinary professional growth and learning for Julie. Assigned by her program there to work with the police academy, Julie was to embark on a life-changing experience. A bit terrified by the prospect of working with this very new and very different community of learners, Julie began a program in educating herself about what to do next. Student engagement, instructional curriculum and objectives, assessment goals and, yes, an ongoing collaborative research project with colleagues there led her on to a path which, until today, still unfolds. Julie has traveled to a half-dozen countries doing workshops and providing consultative services; she has become an internationally recognized expert in English for security specialists. Who knew that would happen? Nobody!

Milestones come in different packaging and Julie's package came out of a sense of extreme malaise and boredom with a job that would have been for others a good one. But she needed a change and she knew it. And she was brave enough to take the risk required to jump in to this very new subspecialty area of English for police officers in Indonesia.

Story 2: When Parents Get Old and You're Far Away

In 2005, we arrived in Hong Kong from Dubai in the middle of a typhoon and the plane struggled to land with many onboard semi-emergencies on the way into Hong Kong Airport. A week later, I started my new job in Hong Kong where I had signed a two-year contract. Three months later, I was comfortably settled in to this extraordinary and challenging new job when my home phone rang in the middle of the night at my new, beautiful, and now almost completely decorated apartment on campus in Senior Staff Quarters. It was my father in upstate New York. "Liz! I'll be over in an hour." "Dad," I mumbled, "it's two o'clock in the morning and I'm in Hong Kong. What are you doing?" "Well, I had a problem with the car and I'm not sure what to do. It won't start! I'll just walk over to your house!" A week later, Dad was diagnosed with Alzheimer's disease and dementia with admission recommended by the doctors to an assisted care facility. For me, what followed were many sleepless nights and great worry – far from home. Finally, I reluctantly decided to break my contract and made plans to head home in two more months, at the end of the semester. And while this milestone can only be described as an unexpected life crisis, these unexpected and unplanned events sent me on a road I never expected to travel, allowing for growth and personal satisfaction. Moving closer to home, I was recruited for and took a job as the director of an established online TESOL graduate program where I learned about administration, teaching, and learning in this innovative way. With my work in online TESOL, this milestone helped me to write a new chapter in my own TESOL career path. I had the opportunity to work with many extraordinarily gifted graduate students. I wrote several articles and book chapters and I edited a volume on the subject of online TESOL. In short, my entire career path took an extraordinary and positive turn.

Many TESOLers work far away from where our parents and family members live. And we struggle to manage family and work responsibilities from a distance. We find ways to do that; and sometimes, we even benefit from it!

Story 3: Can't Buy Me Love

"I'm going to take a job in Saudi Arabia," the text said. "What?!" I responded. Cory had been teaching English while he completed his PhD in applied linguistics. He was interested in online teaching and even took on an adjunct contract so he could make extra money. But even with the overwork, Cory was struggling to make ends meet. I worried about him – a young, single man heading out to a country so very different from his own (United States). What would happen to him? Would he get in trouble? And how would he manage with his outgoing, innovative approach to TESOL professional projects in a program in a new country that seemed to be, as he called it, "pretty traditional?" After three years, Cory had paid off his student debt; and more importantly, he'd found his life partner when he met a nurse after breaking a bone and going to the hospital in the city where he worked. Now, with their son, Cory and his wife enjoy a life filled with love, and yes, hard work too, as they anticipate another move to another country soon.

88 Rewards and Milestones

As this story illustrates, the need for money often drives us in TESOL to take risks. Cory's risk-taking was a gift that will keep on giving for the rest of his life – and that of his wife and son, too. His decision to take this job in Saudi Arabia led Cory on a new path – both personally and professionally – and the benefits are innumerable. Adding to his PhD (and the knowledge and skills that he'd acquired earning it), Cory learned to speak (some) Arabic, learned to work effectively in a university in another country, with people whose daily lives and professional outlook differed dramatically from his own. Cory will write the book on the details; but here, it is easy to see, I hope, that risk-taking can come from a desire to pay the bills; and it doesn't always turn out poorly! Cory's is definitely a story of a TESOL career path reward!

My own rewards and milestones are many; yours are too. Here, I would like to recount three rewards and three milestones. The purpose of the selections below is to offer readers examples from which they will hopefully consider their rewards and milestones and start their own lists.

Three professional rewards are as follows:

1. In 2002, the Teachers of English to Speakers of Other Languages International Association (TESOL.org) gave me the D. Scott Enright Service Award. It was in recognition to my service to the Interest Sections in TESOL and it was a great day for me – one I will never forget. The network of colleagues and the skills set acquired over the preceding years were enough to make me feel appreciated. But this formal recognition of my efforts was what I carry with me today and will carry for my whole life. So grateful for this reward.
2. The completion of my doctoral studies in 1984 led me on a career path that has been truly satisfying in all respects. However, I list my PhD as a "reward" here because it was then and is today a symbol of my sense of value, self-esteem, and legitimacy as a professional. I have felt profound sense of appreciation based on my use of knowledge, skills, and experiences associated with this educational credential. From the confidence I have in a rock-solid foundation in TESOL and the skills I've had in pulling up bits of that foundation to address what are often complex professional problems, I very often feel the sense of "reward" that my doctorate brings and has brought to me at every stage of my career. I have included my PhD as both a reward and as a milestone (see below) because in all ways, it is both. Do you have in your professional past an event that you count as both as a reward and as a milestone?
3. This reward is a collection of messages received and archived in a folder I keep on my laptop desktop. I call it "Liz: Don't Forget These!" In that folder is a collection of notes, photographs, and published snippets collected since I first started engaging in active e-mail correspondence in the late 1990s. Mostly remembrances from former students and colleagues, thank you from

those I've helped with tenure and promotion applications, research grant applications support, letters of reference for graduate school admission, and a host of other messages. It is highly likely that one of you, reading this page right now, have a message in that folder. Last count there were over 300 items in that folder. I hope my laptop never crashes (though, now, these, and other documents are saved in "the cloud."). For me, these "rewards" are a reminder of the impact I have made on the world of English language teaching; and when I am feeling somehow disconnected or otherwise am in need of a reminder of my life's work, I can just open that folder and find a collection of examples. My sincere thanks to all those whose career paths you have shared with me; it's a reward and it's a big one.

Three professional milestones are as follows:

1. Completion of doctoral degree – While I have listed this one in "rewards," I want to illustrate how one life event can sometimes be both a reward and milestone. A doctoral degree, for me, had nothing to do with prestige. In fact, in my home community among members of my extended family (except for two, identified in the front matter of this volume), my achievement of this hard-won reward was viewed as a waste of time. I received no money and no emotional support from anyone for this effort. But perhaps for that reason, I persisted. Many others around me were supportive, kind, and trusting in their confidence in my ability to do this; and it is for that reason I consider my doctoral degree to be a milestone. We achieve milestones against odds sometimes. Odds were against me and I succeeded anyway. In addition, this milestone opened doors that were to shape my professional and personal identity throughout my career.

2. American University in Cairo (AUC) job – I went to Cairo in 1984 with then seven-year-old Sam. The decision to accept a job as Visiting Assistant Professor at the AUC was an uneasy and challenging one. With little knowledge of what I was doing (besides getting on the academic track with my first doctoral level job), a promise by AUC of free housing, excellent schooling for Sam, and a plane ticket for each of us, and with the blessing and encouragement of my doctoral committee members and graduate student colleagues, I leapt off of that cliff in August 1984. I've never regretted having done it, though at the time it seemed like I had done the wrong thing – taking my son away to this completely foreign, unknown place, having significant (almost debilitating) doubts about my ability to navigate teaching at the postgraduate level in this new environment, and a myriad of other worries plagued me. But there we were, at Kennedy Airport, where we took the flight of our lives. Little did I know then that flight and that first trip to Cairo was going to change my life and that of my son's too forever.

90 Rewards and Milestones

At AUC, I learned so much – too much to write here – about teaching, working, raising a child, and a lot of other things. That job and those two years (1984–1986) in Cairo was to have opened doors for future consultancies as well as long-term, tenure line jobs, and research. I was to receive invitations and complete projects in more than 30 countries where the skills learned at AUC came into play – working with Arabic speakers, addressing issues where religion and education intersect, and understanding the intricacies of studying and working in unfamiliar contexts and foreign countries. Returning to AUC for a second contract 2001–2005 was an opportunity to revisit and update my skills and knowledge. During those years and afterward too, I published articles, book chapters, and books on topics emanating from the experience of a total of six years at AUC, including two chapters in a series of two edited volumes on Arabic language teaching (Wahba, Taha, & England, 2006, 2012). Egypt remains deep in my heart today, these 30 years later; and I visit as often as possible to reconnect with my beloved second home, Cairo. In addition, my son's career was dramatically shaped by his experience there as well in that today, he holds an associate professorship in Arabic language and literature. I have many things for which to thank AUC for having brought me to Cairo in 1984.

3. A series of extraordinary professional trips worldwide combine as my third professional milestone: the results gleaned from my participation in two United States Department of State and Georgetown University cosponsored programs: English Language Specialist (EL Spec) and English Language Fellows (ELF). I summarize a few important milestones (taken from a longer list) here in an effort to show how milestones can "amass," and build up over time, one building on another.

   a. EL Spec: In 2008, I made my first trip on an EL Spec program to Pakistan, a country to which I was destined to visit on three assignments. I had completed several other EL Spec programs elsewhere starting in 1992 in Czech Republic. In 2008, the Regional English Language Officer and I traveled to Peshawar, Lahore, and then to Bahawalpur before heading to Islamabad to board a plane for Afghanistan. Needless to say, my work there was a new and in all cases, positive and rich experience. Still, I was new to the region and to the world of teacher education there. A second opportunity came only five years later in 2013, when I again went to Pakistan and discovered (a) what I had done well and was therefore invited back to the same institution to build on what we'd done five years earlier, and (b) what I couldn't do because I didn't know enough to dig deep on some important issues and new security issues and personnel changes. A third opportunity came in 2018, when I made my third Specialist trip to Pakistan, and where I was finally able to work with "Society for Pakistani English Teachers (SPELT) travelling English teachers conference" which took me to Karachi, Islamabad, and Lahore. Because of the serendipitous nature and good fortune of receiving invitations for these three trips – taken at three different stages of my career path, I was able to learn many new strategies, techniques, and content, as well as to contribute in ways that were different each time. My gratitude to the EL Spec Program for its confidence in me and for the opportunities to complete these three programs in Pakistan (and several others worldwide as well). I learned as much from EL Spec as I learned in a graduate course in my doctoral program! Here's the short list: (1) how to work, joke, teach new ideas, engage participants, gain trust, and transform hostile audiences; (2) how to maintain a sense of identity and confidence in the face of a highly charged (in many cases, intensely masculine) meeting; (3) manage food poisoning and a very fully packed schedule of presentations and meetings; and (4) acknowledge and see up close the extraordinary impact of diplomacy (hard and soft) on the ground.

b. ELF: Please note that I have taken liberties here with names. In recent years, there has been a big push to avoid calling us "ELFs." Instead, we're supposed to say "English Language Fellows." But it's my book so I'm using my own (and many others of us) preferred terms!

I received a sabbatical leave award from Shenandoah University, where I was a professor. For my sabbatical project, I accepted an invitation as an ELF in Indonesia, 2012–2013. According to their website, ELFs do this: Through the English Language Fellow (EL Fellow) Program, highly qualified US educators in the field of Teaching English to Speakers of Other Languages (TESOL) or Teaching English as a Foreign Language (TEFL) participate in ten-month-long fellowships at academic institutions throughout the world (English Language Fellow Program, n.d.) https://exchanges.state.gov/us/program/english-language-fellow-program

My ELF assignment – labeled "hard to fill" – took me to a university in the fourth largest city in Indonesia, Makassar, in South Sulawesi. During my 10-month long assignment, I was assigned to teach in a university and lead workshops, seminars, camps, and meetings that took me on 19 trips around Indonesia and I accepted two addendum assignments for trips to Thailand and Malaysia, where I completed short-term teacher education assignments as well. Having felt some confidence from my years in the Middle East, I assumed wrongly that I was completely prepared to address the challenges of working in this new environment in Indonesia. With a crash course in Bahasa Indonesia (the official national language), I set out to conquer my new world. Soon, I learned that I was only partially prepared to complete my assignment. With many rewards,

92 Rewards and Milestones

the challenges were equal in number: the living conditions were difficult for me; the collegial relationships were completely different from those I'd know elsewhere; and the reporting scheme to my superiors was different from what I had previously known. I learned many important professional lessons there as a veteran teacher. Here are three learnings: (1) I don't know how to teach 900 students, which was my original assignment; (2) my intolerance for drinking water shortages is a deal breaker; and (3) leaning on others, even students, is OK. Final reflection: I learned as much from my beloved Indonesian friends, students, and colleagues as I did ever before in my own country, in Egypt or anywhere. Applied to different settings elsewhere, my ELF experience was the hardest job I ever loved. Thank you from the bottom of my heart to everyone who made that year possible for me. For the past six years, since returning home, I have thought every single day about something I learned in Indonesia. And I will cherish the memory of this extraordinary milestone for the rest of my life.

Note: I just counted and as of today, I counted 33 rewards and 13 milestones in my journal. How many of both can you list in yours?

Recommendations

We need to reflect upon and record our rewards and milestones in TESOL. While most of us add those to our resumes, there's more to it than that. Who reads resumes in detail anymore? Rather, recording rewards and milestones can help us to be intentional about and to practice self-care. Taking time out on a relatively regular schedule to think about small successes in our work lives can be a powerful exercise in avoiding burnout. Keeping a record of rewards and milestones can help us to see, over time, what we have accomplished, how we have grown, what we have learned, and how we might go forward in the future. In Chapter 10, I will address in more depth the concept of "'intentionalizing' our career path development." A first step is keeping a record of rewards and milestones. What rewards have you known in your career? How have those pushed you forward on your path? What personal and professional milestones have come your way? And how have you used what you've learned from those to move forward? Have you used a milestone to launch an entrepreneurial project? Did you ask for a raise or a new class to teach? Did a nagging research question turn into a team project with your colleagues, leading then to a presentation at a conference or a publication? Did a church-sponsored service project end up turning into a part- or full-time job for you or for someone you mentored? What have you done, as Mary Oliver describes it "with your one wild and precious life?" Think about it. Write it down. See how rewards and milestones have guided you.

In the final two chapters of this book, I want to offer some thoughts and actions for moving forward as we live our extraordinary lives in TESOL. What can we do next? Chapter 9 addresses "The Roles of Educational Institutions and

Professional Associations for Intentional TESOL Career Path Development," outlining a way forward for larger scale changes and adjustments to our professional career paths with institutional work and professional association efforts. And Chapter 10, "Moving Forward – It's On Us: Teaching, Research and Service for Intentional TESOL Career Path Development," will hopefully help readers to launch their plans for career path development. Together, we can do this.

References

Elton, C. (2009). *The carrot principle: How the best managers use their strengths to engage their people, retain talent and accelerate performance.* New York: Free Press.

England, L. (2006). Methodology in Arabic language teacher education. *Handbook for Arabic language teaching professionals in the 21st century*, 419–436.

English Language Fellow Program (n.d.). Retrieved from https://exchanges.state.gov/us/program/english-language-fellow-program

English Language Specialist Program (n.d.). Retrieved from https://exchanges.state.gov/us/program/english-language-specialist-program

Johnson, B. (2019). *Putting teachers first. How to inspire, motivate and connect with your staff.* New York: Routledge Taylor & Francis.

Kahn, D. L., & Katz, D. (1952). *Leadership practices in relation to productivity.* Ann Arbor, MI: The University of Michigan Social Research Center.

Mana, M., & England, L. (2017). Proposing professional standards for Arabic teacher certification. In Wahba, K. M., Taha, Z. A., & England, L. (Eds.) *Handbook for Arabic language teaching professionals in the 21st century, Volume II* (pp. 361–372). New York: Routledge.

Wahba, K., England, L., & Taha, Z. (2017). *Handbook for Arabic Language Teaching Professionals in the 21st Century. Volume II.* New York: Routledge Taylor & Francis. https://doi.org/10.4324/9781315676111

Wahba, K., Taha, Z., & England, L. (2006). *Handbook for Arabic language teaching professionals in the 21st century* (1st ed). New York: Lawrence Erlbaum. https://doi.org/10.4324/9780203824757

9

MOVING FORWARD – ROLES OF EDUCATIONAL ORGANIZATIONS AND LANGUAGE TEACHERS ASSOCIATIONS

What Is "Intentional" TESOL Career Path Development?

We know from Chapter 1 that TESOL (Teachers of English to Speakers of Other Languages) career path development is a description of how individuals proceed in their professional lives. As an interdisciplinary concept, TESOL career path development draws on work in language teacher education, teacher motivation, leadership, organizational development, and life balance. While much of what we do in our TESOL careers relies on the forces of luck, serendipity, and good fortune, I wish to introduce the concept of "intentionality" to TESOL career path development. "Intentional TESOL career path development" is a systematic effort to take control of, to purposefully and deliberately address how we develop professionally, from preservice to novice, then to mid-career/career switcher, veteran, and finally, semiretired.

By making regular assessments of what we have to offer, what we know, and what we can do, our paths are more satisfying, less startling, and traumatic when changes occur, and a lot more fun. A verbally stated aim or plan, combined with a reasonable path forward can be an extraordinary experience for any TESOLer. I'd like to suggest that we make it mandatory for all of us! Caution here: It doesn't mean that one sets out at the tender age of 22 for what she/he will do for the rest of their lives. Rather, such self-assessments offer TESOLers the opportunity to own their professional identities in ways that "just letting it happen" might not. Too often, TESOLers lay blame on others for their professional misfortunes. And there are times when others are responsible for our difficulties or failures. But taking the step that includes setting goals and taking aim can be a first step toward avoiding being at the mercy of others. Start today to establish your TESOL career path! In Chapter 10, I will outline some suggested routes for doing that. Here, we will explore ways in which workplaces and language teacher associations can help in ways they have not always done.

How Can Workplace Settings Help Teachers Throughout Our Careers?

In this book, I focus squarely on teachers and how they move forward along their career paths. In the next section, I hope to modify the usual approach to workplace teacher support, refocus attention and hopefully, prepare the way for research and development for teachers at all stages of their careers.

The usual approach to workplace teacher support includes supervisors (and others in powerful positions) to identify and correct teacher weaknesses and lack of knowledge and/or skill creating training and other professional development plans (often with little or no teacher input, no compensation and high expectations). The approach presented here includes ways in which workplace settings can actually encourage, support and appreciate teacher strengths while at the same time providing training and other support to improve teachers' sense of engagement, commitment, and enthusiasm for their work and for their students.

Teaching, Research, and Service and Teacher Education

Preservice teachers are committed to doing well in their programs of study. Enrolling these individuals means that institutions support them as they begin to establish themselves as TESOL professionals. In some university programs, TESOLers take classes with those in linguistics, bilingual education, multicultural education, and a host of other subspecialty majors. How do these programs work intentionally to support individualized programs of study for TESOLers while helping them to integrate with and learn from those in related fields? How are these preservice TESOLers prepared for their first jobs? As a multidisciplinary field in its own right, TESOL offers other subspecialty areas a general perspective, a research canon, and a professional role identity that can serve other subspecialty fields as well. How do TESOL graduate students acquire their professional identities and how do they learn to share their knowledge and skills with those in related fields? Graduate programs serve their students. And graduate-level, preservice teacher education programs and accrediting bodies that sanction their activities must address these questions.

Novice/beginners teachers rely on their preservice experiences as they start their first professional teaching jobs. What do the programs that hire them do to support these teachers as they enter the world of work?

Mid-career/career switchers offer special skills, services, and challenges to workplace institutions. With their willingness to rely on what they already

96 Educational Organizations and LTAs

know from both their current positions and from previous workplace projects, mid-career and career switcher TESOLers have instructional teaching assignments and leadership roles in curriculum, assessment, and accreditation initiatives. Mid-career and career switcher TESOLers need support to achieve high standards for student performance and for their own professional development too. Institutions serve mid-career and career switcher employees through their efforts to manage reasonable workloads, training on new instructional initiatives and other projects, and support for teacher and classroom-based research. Teachers at this stage of their career paths need and deserve policies and programs that are intentionally designed to retain those teachers. Those policies and programs include financial support for strong employment benefits packages, conference attendance, and participation and policies that identify and intentionally promote the professional expertise of mid-career and career switcher TESOLers. Sabbatical and other leave policies contribute to those efforts.

Veteran teachers have a tendency to focus on detail, organization, and material concerns more than on work. They can handle anything – discipline problems, scheduling conflict, assessment challenges, and the necessary "juggling act" required to get through the days and weeks of the semester. More than other stages and relying on their deep knowledge of institutional culture and procedures, veteran teachers are squarely focused on their programs and their own professional lives. Institutional support for veteran teachers might include ongoing professional development programs that provide veterans with opportunities to reach out elsewhere – to learn new skills and tools, to interact and engage with other academic and professional communities, and to be models and mentors for TESOLers who are novice/beginners and mid-career/career switchers.

Semiretired TESOLers offer continuity and mature values and wisdom. Their contributions depend on their availability, the program administration's willingness to include them in relevant projects, and how they interact with students and full-time faculty and staff. In the current description, semiretired means "part-time"; and so the depth of engagement of semiretirees is lesser than for the previous four phases that are (here) full-time positions. Institutional support for semiretirees include engaging and utilizing semiretirees' knowledge and skills to support the efforts of those other teachers in the preceding four groups. As with veterans, semiretired TESOLers provide opportunities for programs as mentors, change agents, and leadership support. No longer, at least in the United States, does advanced age mean advanced position on the job. The part-time 80+ year old founder of the institution might come in to work only two days a week. And the vice president is 29 years old, while those who work for her are, for example, 40–60 years old. Semiretirees must learn to work in new employment settings from the past, when older meant higher on the org chart. How do institutions manage this new world of employment and age differences? How

Educational Organizations and LTAs **97**

can semiretirees contribute to their workplaces in this new environment? In more traditional workplace environments, semiretired professionals will also face challenges, as they learn how to support younger, newer supervisors.

One author has noted that for the first time in history, institutions in the United States might hire employees in four generations! And unlike the case in many other countries, advanced age does not guarantee an advanced position. So, for example, one might find a 29-year-old vice president supervising the 84-year-old institutional founder; and a 60-year-old lifelong teacher might have a supervisor ten or even 20 years younger than he is. In short, the complexities of workplace communications and the place of those in the "semiretired" phase (indeed, those in all phases) are changing dramatically. How does a semiretiree take leadership instructions from a 29-year-old boss? How can the 60-year-old engineer who has spent his entire career in the same job now take orders from a boss who is only slightly older than his daughter? The times they are a-changin' for TESOLers and those in other professions too as the workplace becomes increasingly diverse and where older may no longer mean the same as "higher in rank" (or higher paycheck).

How Can Professional Associations Help Teachers Throughout Our Careers?

Professional language teacher association based initiatives worldwide (local, regional, national, and international) are in place now to support TESOLers worldwide in their efforts to move intentionally along their career paths. While published work focuses mostly on professional teaching associations, there are a number of organized efforts outside the structure of formal associations as well. What I hope to address in this chapter is a collection of hopeful signs for us all – both those within Language Teaching Associations (LTAs) and outside of those to work more effectively to help teachers intentionally throughout their careers and to expand the reach of the LTA's mission.

Preservice Teachers

Preservice teachers (often students in training to be English language teachers in the future) worldwide are members of associations where there are sometimes designated subgroups focusing on the needs of preservice (graduate) students in TESOL and related fields. TESOL International Association, for example, enjoys a robust year-round electronic communications addressing topics of interest to preservice teachers – those writing graduate-level theses, seeking jobs, and other topics. With the Master's considered the "terminal degree" in teaching English to speakers of other languages, emphasis is on those seeking that degree or a higher one (PhD or EdD).

What LTAs might do for Preservice Teachers?

Worldwide, of course, many teachers find employment in TESOL with a bachelor's degree and sometimes even less formal education. With the total number of English teachers worldwide currently only a matter of speculation with few reliable sources of data, I report here from an article published in 2015 by Freeman, Katz, Garcia Gomez, and Burns, "There are, by current estimates, some 15 million teachers of English around the world" (p. 10). And in addition, Canagarajah (1999) writes, "... more than 80% of the ELT professionals internationally are non-native speakers." (p. 91). That means that there are about 12 million non-native English-speaking teachers (NNESTs) around the world. Addressing career path development for native and non-native English teachers is the business of organizations that employ us as well as language teaching associations that seek to address our professional needs. In a presentation at the annual meeting, the Executive Director, Christopher Powers (2019), said that TESOL International Association's membership total was 10,944 members.

There is a huge number of teachers worldwide who are not members of TESOL International Association. Serving those preservice teachers – the majority of them worldwide, I would argue – is a worthy effort for language teaching associations. Here are a few suggestions for those who may want to address this glaring omission in TESOL preservice efforts on the part of LTAs.

1. Prioritizing teacher education for preservice teachers through university partnerships in large, undeserved areas, LTAs might provide online teacher training programs, where Internet access is unavailable or weak, paper-based materials might be provided to those universities.
2. In collaboration with accreditation bodies, LTAs might collect data on the preservice English language teacher education programs worldwide.

Novice/Beginners Teachers

Beginning teachers find excellent support with language teacher associations. With hundreds of presentations each year at the international convention, TESOL International Association addresses the professional developmental needs of teachers who may be in their first year or very early in their TESOL careers. While the emphasis of most conference presentations is on classroom and online teaching and language learning, and less on ways in which teachers are served on their career paths, novice teachers find great professional developmental opportunities at TESOL conventions worldwide. International conferences offer a variety of additional program opportunities, including plenary speeches, exhibitions with books and other materials available for teachers, employment clearing house, and various private and government-sponsored programs for novice English language teachers. National conferences provide (usually annual) opportunities for novice teachers from across a country to meet and share knowledge and teaching and learning tools with one another and with teachers at other stages of their careers. And regional conferences are great opportunities for those novice teachers to learn more about rewards and challenges in a closer, more familiar geographical area. And finally, local conferences are often held to address a specific theme of relevance to novice teachers who are new both to teaching and to the local area.

What might be offered to novice teachers by LTAs?

1. Address the tendency of novices to overwork themselves. Teach basic "whole person" skills and present models for teacher collaboration on significant projects.
2. Create ways for novices to address "the hazing experience" (Farrell, 2012) in professional development. For example, offer workshops and presentations for mid-career and veteran teachers on how to manage novice teachers: tendency to overwork and need for professional support in focusing their energy and enthusiasm on useful projects.

Mid-Career/Career Switchers

Perhaps the most poorly supported TESOLers are the mid-career/career switcher teachers. They may, in general, disengage from professional development opportunities offered by LTAs. For those who attend these, it would appear that they feel less than satisfied with the content. I know of no data to support this claim; however, I have heard from former students and colleagues for decades that their decision to switch out of TESOL careers was in some part based on the fact that they don't feel that their professional needs are met in the context of conferences or other LTA efforts that address a somewhat narrow approach to TESOL content. Whether it is the teacher, himself/herself is at fault or if it's the LTA that should be held accountable for those who are generally dissatisfied, many teachers at mid-career often hold leadership positions and are responsible for program content – curriculum, assessment, and a variety of administrative roles. And their sense of engagement and level of morale are critical factors in overall program function. LTAs might do more for TESOLers at this phase of their career paths.

What might LTAs do to support mid-career/career switcher teachers?

1. Create professional projects specifically designed to attract and engage mid-career TESOLers. Some examples (already in place) might be revised and built upon: mentoring programs, large-scale research projects (see preservice above), and teacher exchange programs.

100 Educational Organizations and LTAs

2. Partner with sister associations to learn more about "related fields" and build bridges to enhance employment opportunities for mid-career/career switcher TESOLers.
3. Address causes, symptoms, and treatment of professional career burnout.

Veterans

Veteran TESOLers have turned a professional corner. They have often moved away from the idealism that drove them earlier in their careers to focus now more on personal concerns more than work, on material benefits over intrinsic motives. Their strong skills in the classroom and in online teaching, in organizing and leading sustain them in the workplace. However, they are also the "top earners"; and they are at higher risk of being demoted or fired and replaced with less expensive appointees or junior colleagues. Some feel that they have given their professional lives to TESOL and now, with highly specialized skills, they perceive themselves to have few career options. They want something back. LTAs can support these teachers. I would argue, in fact, that our associations owe these teachers. Most have contributed greatly to their programs and to the LTAs as well.

What might LTAs do to support veteran teachers?

1. Harness the expertise of veteran teachers. With mature values, honed skills, historical memory, and commitment to the profession, veteran TESOLers offer knowledge, skills and habits that serve the association's mission. LTAs might leverage that knowledge and those skills in a variety of ways: by hosting regular electronic meetings wherein veteran teachers might work out issues that they face, share resources and rewards and challenges too. And TESOLers at other stages of their career paths – preservice, novice, and mid-career/career switchers – might participate in an intentional way to address career path issues with these veteran teachers. Veteran teachers might be tapped to serve as liaisons with other professional communities where English language teachers' skills and knowledge are needed.
2. Provide membership benefits to meet the needs of veteran teachers – group insurance policies, financial aid services, and elder care services.
3. Address causes, symptoms, and treatment of professional career burnout.

Semiretireds

Semiretired TESOLers serve their professional associations in a variety of ways: heading up association initiatives (usually, this role relies at least partly on "name recognition" of the semiretiree), leadership roles within the association, and some mentoring. More relaxed than their veteran teacher colleagues, semiretired TESOLers enjoy part-time teaching and other projects.

And finally, what might LTAs do to support semiretired teachers?

Another underserved group, semi-retired TESOLers have much to offer those at other stages of their career paths. Here, I am afraid I will creep into the world of "anecdote," stories from my own (recent) professional communications and efforts with former students, colleagues, program directors, and others. What can TESOL International Association do for semiretired TESOLers? A lot more!

1. Create guidelines for volunteerism. Semiretired TESOLers, and indeed those at other phases of their careers too, provide volunteer help in numerous programs and in their communities as well. We need better information on what might be "volunteer work" and what work might be considered "professional," thus worthy of a fee-based professional contract agreement. In my experience, TESOLers provide professional services and are expected to do it gratis, for free. And while one never turns down a friend asking for career advice, there are times when volunteerism can be abused. What is TESOL volunteerism? How can our professional associations help us to know what makes for legitimate paid work?

2. Offer support for employment issues and job-based discrimination. TESOL International Association has addressed some employment-related issues (the discriminatory employment practice of not hiring non-native English speaking teachers being the most notable). But for years, TESOL International Association has danced around employment issues.

As a nonprofit association, there's been a lot of worry over fiduciary responsibility and the critical importance of the association's steering clear of employment- or labor-related issues. This timidity has created opportunities that would not otherwise be available for employers to abuse TESOL members. I got fired without notice and with evidence of neither incompetence nor wrongdoing. Why didn't I get tenure when lesser productive colleagues and researchers did? What do I do if my boss sexually harasses me? How can I address this instance of bullying at work? Why are meetings I schedule with my boss always canceled by him and never rescheduled? These are just some employment questions that I have come across in the past year. More support for employment-related problems should be available from LTAs.

What Kinds of Professional Career Path Development Are Going on Outside of Academic Institutions and Workplace and Professional Associations?

In this chapter, we have focused on both workplace and professional association based professional development opportunities for TESOLers. Where else can we find opportunities for progressing in TESOL? In my interviews with teachers,

102 Educational Organizations and LTAs

here's a partial list of those resources. We all know they're out there. It's time to identify and engage these in order to show how other, less formal and more anecdotal connections improve and enrich our professional lives:

1. Churches, community-based organizations, and non-governmental organizations that support non-native English speakers and those who serve them. Many of us are fortunate to live in communities where these opportunities present themselves. Recently, the public school system in my own small city in Virginia invited me to take a leadership role in the design, implementation, and evaluation of a first-ever dual language program in English and Spanish. I found it to be an extraordinary and life-changing milestone in my own professional life. The various university practicum students, colleagues, and parents we invited in and who joined the school staff in building the program also grew and changed as a result of this experience. Working in service roles with refugees and those non-native English speakers with disabilities and interrupted educations can be as gratifying for their teachers and helpers as it is for those learners themselves. Another teacher reports on presentations she has been called on to make for a local retirement and assisted living facility following her short-term contract work with English teachers overseas. Those talks and workshops led her to a new career in music therapy for geriatric patients.

   There are many ways in which to serve one's community and at the same time, learn and change oneself.
2. In professions and academic disciplines that are closely connected to us in TESOL, we can find opportunities for professional career path development. One former student was hired as a tutor to work with a newly arrived non-native English-speaking corporate executive. Navigating a new corporate culture after having worked mainly in schools, this novice TESOLer gained experience and confidence in a related field. Within the context of those who hire TESOL-educated professionals, there is a long list of "closely connected fields" where TESOL career paths grow and flourish. How and to what extent can we learn more about how those connections work to provide new directions for TESOLers?

We cannot ignore the power of social media in how well we move through our careers. Facebook, Twitter, and all the other various outlets are changing everything for everyone in TESOL at all stages of our career paths. Physical distances are no longer a deal-breaker when it comes to networking, learning about how it is to teach in a faraway country, and even taking free classes with massive open online courses (MOOCs) – all of these and others too are new. Some, particularly those who were educated prior to the Internet-based explosion of information and communication resources, will struggle to include these in their networking. After all, those who were educated in the more traditional, face-to-face approach will find social networking to be lacking, difficult to navigate and unsatisfying. To them, I say "Don't worry! You're not alone!" I encourage all TESOLers and all who may be reading this who consider themselves to be outside of the TESOL world and are not yet connected on social media, to try Facebook for one day – set up an account and type "TESOL" into the search box. See what's there. I would venture that all will find something to like. Build your professional network on social media. If you don't like Facebook, fine; try another outlet. But get connected – you will very likely end up liking something about it and you will definitely learn something new.

In summary, roles are changing, for both those education-oriented organizations hiring TESOL professionals as well as the roles of professional associations for teachers. But what happens next, individually, for ESL (English as a Second Language) programs and for our professional world – what happens next is on us. In Chapter 10, I will offer a list of ways to be more conscious of and careful about our efforts to move forward in TESOL. I call it "intentionalizing" our career paths.

References

Canagarajah, A. S. (1999). Interrogating the "native speaker fallacy": non-linguistic roots, non-pedagogical results. In G. Braine (Ed.), *Non-native educators in English language teaching* (pp. 77–92). Mahwah, NJ: Erlbaum.

Farrell, T. S. C. (2012). Novice-service language teacher development: Bridging the gap between preservice and in-service education and development. *TESOL Quarterly, 46*(3), 435–449. https://doi.org/10.1002/tesq.36

Freeman, D., Katz, A., Garcia Gomez, P., & Burns, A. (2015). English-for-teaching: Rethinking teacher proficiency in the classroom. *ELT Journal, 69*(2). https://doi.org/10.1093/elt/ccu074

Powers, C. (2019, March 15). Presentation at TESOL International Association Convention Annual Business Meeting, Atlanta, GA.

10

IT'S ON US: INTENTIONAL TESOL CAREER PATH DEVELOPMENT

Overview

What I hope to illustrate and confirm here is this: No one else is going to pave our paths for us. It's our job to make sure we have whatever it takes – knowledge, skills, habits, moral courage, and grit – to move ahead. Whatever your philosophy of life, religious beliefs, and faith may be – we have to go forward; the world was not created so we could go back. Sometimes, we want to go back. We dream of the past, the good ol' days. I do it all the time – drawing on my many positive memories. But in reality, we have to go forward. Our TESOL (Teachers of English to Speakers of Other Languages) career paths take us along, like it or not. And my message is this: It's on us! No one else is going to make our lives fulfilled and happy. We might as well figure it out, plan as best as we can and most of all, enjoy it!

A Personal Note

I've had a remarkable career! In fact, my career path and the many colleagues, friends, and former students who've encouraged me to do everything, including the writing of this book, have been the most significant force behind my decisions! In one early review of the manuscript proposal, one reader said "The author wants to write a book about her own extraordinary career!" Well, yes and no. I wanted to write about ways of elevating and promoting all of our career paths. But that reviewer was right and for the curious, here's my career path (the short version):

I began my TESOL career teaching ESL (English as a Second Language) to Vietnamese refugees (in Madison, Wisconsin, in December 1975); next, I taught graduate students-to-be at Georgia Tech (mostly Iranians and Colombians in 1978–1980). In 1980, I entered a doctoral program at University of Illinois Champaign-Urbana and four short years later, with my brand new PhD and seven-year-old son, I went to Egypt in 1984 to teach in the Master's in TEFL (Teaching English as a Foreign Language) and TAFL (Teaching Arabic as a Foreign Language) programs at the American University in Cairo. Returning in 1986, I had a one-year job at Southern Illinois University, followed by seven hard years at Eastern Michigan University (granted tenure in 1993 and resigned in 1994, yes, from a tenured job). I did some consulting and then joined a private language school (now closed) as Chief Academic Officer, updating their curriculum at 17 schools and universities in the United States and two elsewhere. After two years of successful and completed curriculum revision work and a lot of travel (domestic and international), including trips to manage the steps in the curriculum overhaul for all (17 then) school programs nationwide and in Germany, I was suddenly (and surprisingly) fired. I moved on next to a small private college as Chair of English as a Second Language. I was terminated from that job, filed a labor dispute with several other colleagues, and got a settlement (one never really wins a law suit). In any case, I learned a lot about United States labor laws, academic politics, and how those intersect (and don't) with legal practice and culture – knowledge I'd never had previously, certainly not in any formal setting. I gained a keen awareness of the value of advocacy skills (and learned too of my particular skill at effectively using that knowledge for my own benefit) and self-care. I have been able to pass those along to others too. Back to Cairo in August 2001 for four years as Visiting Associate Professor (when the World Trade Center bombings happened three weeks later, I was sitting in my apartment in Cairo – another story, but a key element for what was to be four more years in Cairo and ever after) and then to Hong Kong for a year in 2005. My father took ill and I reluctantly left Hong Kong (I am grateful to those who graciously allowed me to break my contract and who held my hand through this very difficult period) and returned to the United States as TESOL Chair at Shenandoah University, leading an established online TESOL graduate degree and certificates program, from where I retired in 2016. Since then, I have been teaching ESL part-time at a local community college, consulting with K-12 schools and some international consulting, TESOL association leadership work, and writing. Yes, indeed, it's been a truly remarkable career for me.

What's left? For now, I take full advantage of social media with daily connections there and by other means with many wonderful colleagues, friends, students, and supporters worldwide – more than I deserved. And still, yes, there are also, milestones, rewards, and ups and downs, mostly ups. Here's what I have: an extraordinary and multifaceted education to be a teacher, extreme motivation (my doctoral dissertation addressed that topic!), organizations that were key features – supportive and toxic, opportunities to learn leadership – to lead and be led, the value of a balanced life, and I try not to forget the tens of rewards and milestones along the way.

106 It's On Us: Intentional TESOL Career Path Development

What I've learned through all of these jobs and consultancies and from the research done on this book is this (in 125 words!):

> There are three essential career skills for TESOLers beyond the content of graduate degree programs – networking, advocacy, and technology skills. We need to address and embrace these and we need to do that intentionally. "Intentional TESOL career path development" is a systematic effort to take control of, to purposefully and deliberately address how we develop professionally, from preservice to novice, then to mid-career/career switcher, veteran, and finally, semiretired. How do we "intentionalize" our own TESOL careers? Well, we don't do it by focusing only on the content of our classes. We do it by focusing on our whole selves – bodies, minds, and souls – throughout our lives. Here, I build a case for doing that in those three specific areas – networking, advocacy, and technology skills.

Networking

With the help of a large number of people – mostly but not all TESOLers – I have managed to acquire an extraordinary international community of practice (described in my recent contribution to *The TESOL Encyclopedia,* published last year by Wiley). These individuals and groups have guided me as role models, coresearchers, brainstorming partners, therapists, and crisis interventionists. I owe my professional success to these people. Wherever I have gone, my network has grown – connecting as we all do, with some people (not all – there are plenty of those who likely dislike, don't care or misunderstand what I say or write!). I encourage readers to write down the categories of people in their lives whom they consider to be their network. Then, start naming names. List everyone who has supported you and whom you have supported over the course of your career path – however long or short. Engaging in this exercise of listing "My Professional Network – Naming Names" will most likely help you to make decisions for your next steps. In some respects, creating awareness of and documenting our professional networks is the first step in advocacy, which is the next essential skill for TESOLers throughout our careers.

Advocacy

A topic that spans all stages and all factors influencing TESOL career path development, I include this topic as one of the three critical parts of TESOL career path development. "It's On Us ..." focuses the key message of this book – that while we may not have the skills to do so and we may be seeking ways to do better, at the end of the day our career paths are set by us, not by others. And we all need to know advocacy skills. We need to be able to use those skills – more now than ever in the past.

Let's put a larger amount of advocacy in our backpacks as we travel along our TESOL career paths, starting today! I still have a twinge of selfishness when I talk about my experience with the legal fight I mounted when dismissed from my job in 2001 and described above. Teachers often feel selfish when talking about ways of helping themselves, engaging in what we're socialized to think that we aren't supposed to think about ourselves; and in so doing, we've been victimized. We've learned to behave like victims in that we feel guilty if we don't return students' essays at the next class meeting (Palmer, personal communication May 24, 2019). We resist confronting a toxic work environment where a supervisor or colleague is abusive. We avoid getting physical exercise, even when our partners and loved ones and medical doctors tell us to do that. We resist learning how to use new tech tools that come out because we're too busy doing other things for other people. And we ignore our need for balance – even when we know well that we are feeling out of balance. "It's on us" means that we have to take care of ourselves – first, not last; first – not never. Learn a new software package, buy a new laptop or phone, and do some yoga! Self-care begins with self. Go for it!

While there are notable exceptions, particularly in some of the recently developed and distributed web-based materials from the TESOL International Association (for members only), advocacy skills for teachers should be a top priority for TESOL professionals worldwide. Part of the reason for the omission of teachers' voices in language policy and society in general is our profession's failure to help teachers to acquire the skills they need to advocate on their own behalf. To some degree, this book addresses this need and contains what I hope will be useful information for readers to begin to build their advocacy skills. Advocacy is support, backing, championing, arguing for, and pushing for a person or event. Until now, TESOLers have done a better job of advocating on behalf of their students than they have on advocating on behalf of themselves (teachers). More advocacy is needed for TESOLers with infusion of advocacy knowledge, skills, and habits into all academic and workplace-based teacher education programs, pre- and in-service. In addition, advocacy skills development should be relegated not only to teacher education programs; we should create our own advocacy skills development programs for ourselves; and those programs – formal and informal – should extend throughout our careers.

While we know well of advocacy efforts for English language learners and students by government agents, schools and universities and colleges, and language teacher associations, there are relatively few efforts and to my knowledge almost no research on the topic of advocacy for teachers. Intentional focus on

108 It's On Us: Intentional TESOL Career Path Development

advocating on behalf of the professional needs of teachers is minimal or completely omitted in TESOL in all countries worldwide.

What is advocacy? Dictionary definitions vary but the gist is this: Advocacy means public support for or recommendation of a particular cause or policy. In TESOL, advocacy is often paired with social justice and pertains directly to teachers and other professionals to advocate on behalf of students. While a laudable effort, my focus here and in this book is on advocacy for teachers. How can teachers be better advocates for themselves as well as their programs and students? How does the public support and recommend on behalf of teachers? What do local, state and provincial, and national and international bodies do to support teachers on the job? What skills and knowledge constitute advocacy in TESOL? To what extent do we in TESOL prepare teachers with those? Advocacy for self, advocacy for peers, and advocacy for programs in which we are the essential component – all of these types of advocacy and the subskills that are required to address issues demanding teacher advocacy – all of these are essential skills for TESOLers throughout our careers.

More intentional efforts in which teachers acquire skills to advocate on their own behalf will strengthen our profession and our programs. Most of all, *teachers' abilities to advocate on their own behalf* will improve job performance and job satisfaction, while at the same time, enhancing career path development. Peer advocacy is another important skill and ways in which it might be taught and learned will vary with the context; I would not have acquired my own peer advocacy skills without the models, issues, and conflicts my peers have faced and for which I have been fortunate to lend a hand in addressing. Program advocacy usually involves addressing the needs of a particular group of students. Advocating on behalf of English programs almost never intentionally and directly addresses the need nor value of advocating on behalf of teachers.

Based on the research presented in this volume, the following advocacy subskills might be considered as part of all TESOL education and continuing education (Table 10.1). I present these as part of the early theoretical profile (Chapter 2) of five stages in a career path. While emphasis here is stage by stage, all advocacy skills should be focused throughout one's career.

Networking and advocacy are essential skills for TESOLers throughout our careers. But there is another, final, skill set – often left to the good luck or professional networking capacity of TESOLers worldwide – and that is the effective use of technology in our professional communities: teaching, research, and service.

Technology

"Liz, we'll do better when we meet and can talk about this." That was a close friend I've known a long time who called recently to address a complex issue.

It's On Us: Intentional TESOL Career Path Development 109

TABLE 10.1 Advocacy skills for five career stages

Stage	Advocacy skills focus
Preservice	Introduction to TESOL professional advocacy: what is it and how to do it, how to interview for a job you want, finding a mentor, learning how to collaborate, identifying a research topic area of interest, using personal network to find and develop service opportunities
Novice	Awareness of commonalities and differences in advocating on behalf of self, students, and program; avoiding despair; priority setting; coping with high vulnerability and combatting timidity, insecurity
Mid-career and career switcher	Building advocacy effectiveness in teaching, assessment, management, and mentoring; intentional networking and building research cache; specific issue-focused advocacy training: local, regional, national, and international issues; burnout coping skills
Veteran	Being a teacher leader: support for teachers as individuals and community leaders, recognizing ourselves as developing adults, working with highly diverse colleagues and supervisors, and burnout coping skills
Semiretired	Differentiation of volunteer, low-pay, and contract-based services and products; looking forward, not back. Identifying and promote skills acquired through your TESOL career, addressing both professional achievements and impact and personal milestones that have provided you with mature values and new skills. Finally, make a plan for future learning and doing.

"Jay," I cried into the phone after hearing the anxious tone in his voice and assessing quickly how complex this issue was, "We can't meet! You've got to solve this in two days and we live far away from each other." "Oh, yeah," he said after a long silence. "I don't know how to do this online," he confessed. "I can't deal with all this technology anymore!" I tried to gently tell Jay that we could try to work it out on a video conference call, maybe GoToMeeting or Zoom. Silence again. Jay didn't know those words. He'd never done an online meeting. He was at the bottom of bewilderment and he didn't know what to do. "Sorry, Jay," I wanted to say – "It's over! We have to do this using computer-based communications! Get over it!" I wanted to but I didn't. I just listened to him complain about technology for ten more minutes. Poor Jay. Of course, he's not alone. A lot of TESOLers struggle now with new and different ways of communicating on professional issues. In no small part for that very reason, Routledge wanted to publish my book entitled *Online Language Teacher Education – TESOL*

110 It's On Us: Intentional TESOL Career Path Development

Perspectives in 2012. It was the first book to address this topic; and while the content was trend-setting, it was very late coming. We needed that book a long time earlier. Better late than never? In the book, we address the learning, teaching, and administration of online language teacher education programs. I'm indebted to the many contributors of this edited volume who brought forward their own research, experience, and analysis of this important issue. TESOLers worldwide need more and better guidance throughout our careers in how to move from face-to-face to online teaching, learning, and communicating with one another.

No longer can we, who learned languages and completed our degrees in face-to-face settings, rely on the ways in which we carried out professional communications in the classroom, in the office, or anywhere else. Since the late 1990s, the entire TESOL professional world has changed. With the advent of distance learning programs and online teaching and learning, the Internet, e-mail use, cell phone communications, and a myriad of applications for completing meetings, holding workshops, and engaging with colleagues, students, and others on social media. We can't keep pretending that things will change back – that we can print out all those messages and data, and that we'll get paid mileage or fare to drive or fly to a meeting far away.

But there's more to the role of technology for TESOL professional career path development than the content of traditional linguistics-based teacher education. How do we communicate online while engaged in collaborative research projects – research question development, literature reviews, data collection and analysis, decisions on where to publish an article or chapter in a book? These are just a few of the questions that are addressed somewhat but not in depth in our earlier book (England, 2012).

How do we manage professional service projects and committee work that include no familiar face-to-face engagement? What happens when someone gets an e-mail that wasn't supposed to go them? How do we repair a failed message due to Internet having gone down at a critical moment in a curriculum or service project meeting? These and many other issues have yet to be addressed. And these are the content of "effective technology use" in TESOL. "She can teach that app to herself" doesn't work for everyone; maybe it works for very few. We need instruction and mentoring in teaching ourselves professional skills, which might be a part of an overall program in advocacy and/or self-care. Continued omission of technology updates and online communications skills will lead to more teacher burn-out, more and more toxic work environments, and ultimately, less effective programs. While there are exceptions, more varied, relevant, and intentional efforts to teach and update technology applications for TESOL career preparation (both pre- and in-service) are needed. It's on us to learn and be able to communicate effectively using technology in TESOL.

While most of the skills identified here for networking, advocacy, and technology use are in the hands of pre- and in-service teacher education practitioners, we too, individually, carry the burden to identify effective ways to stay current and truly be TESOL professionals throughout our careers. It's on us!

We bring our life to the table when we take a job in TESOL. For TESOLers, we bring our academic knowledge, our professional skills, and our personal identities, habits, and values. We know when we hit the mark, when we do our best. We know when we don't. That sense of comfort and ease when things go well and that nagging, painful sense of loss, failure, or indecision – these are well-known to every TESOLer. I hope in the chapters of this book more TESOLers will find their way through with more of the former and happier days and fewer of the latter and sadder more difficult ones.

We need to be concerned now, urgently, because we're losing ground on our impact and the future depends on our refocusing our efforts to address our career paths – developing networks, building advocacy efforts, and using technology in all its various forms to address the future of our professional community of practice. Please find a detailed description of communities of practice in the 2018 publication (England, 2018, in Liontas, Ed.) We can resist doing it; but that decision will come with a price. To embrace a new approach and committing ourselves to intentional efforts to identify, discuss, and study – that's the TESOL career path development I hope for – for all of us. Many TESOLers are open to this effort. It's time to get this party started. And it's on us to set the time and date for creating the joy and enthusiasm for doing it. Using whatever resonates in this book to encourage you, please join me in taking your first steps.

References

England, L. (Ed.). (2012). *Online language teacher education: TESOL perspectives*. New York City, NY: Routledge Taylor-Francis.

England, L. (2018). Communities of practice. In J. I. Liontas (Ed.), *The TESOL encyclopedia of English language teaching. 8 volume set*. New York, NY: Wiley-Blackwell. https://doi.org/10.1002/9781118784235.eelt0396

REFERENCES

Adoniou, M. (2019). TESOL 2019 Conference (presentation handout), Chicago, IL.

Aguilar, E. (2018). *The onward workbook: Daily activities to cultivate your emotional resilience and thrive.* San Francisco, CA: Jossey Boss.

Amzat, I. H., & Valdez, N. P. (Eds.). (2017). *Teacher empowerment and practices: Perspectives across borders.* Singapore: Springer Singapore.

Anthony, E. M. (1963). Approach, method, and technique. *ELT Journal, 17*(2), 63–67. https://doi.org/10.1093/elt/XVII.2.63

ASCD. (n.d.). *What is teacher leadership?* Retrieved from http://www.ascd.org/publications/books/105048/chapters/What-Is-Teacher-Leadership%C2%A2.aspx

Ashforth, B. E., & R. H. Humphrey (1993). Emotional labor in service roles: The influence of identity. *Academy of Management Review, 8*(1). Retrieved from https://doi.org/10.5465/amr.1993.3997508

Association for Supervision of Curriculum Development. (n.d.). *What is Teacher Leadership?* Retrieved from http://www.ascd.org/publications/books/105048/chapters/What-Is-Teacher-Leadership%C2%A2.aspx

Atchley, R. C. (1971). Retirement and leisure participation: Continuity or crisis? *The Gerontologist, 11*(1), 13–17. https://doi.org/10.1093/geront/11.1_Part_1.13

Augier, M., & Teece, D. J. (2018). *The Palgrave encyclopedia of strategic management living edition.* London, UK: Palgrave Macmillan.

Bailey, M., & WetFeet (Firm). (2006). *Finding the right career path (WetFeet insider guide)* (EBSCO eBook Subscription Academic Collection – North America). San Francisco, CA: WetFeet. Retrieved from https://shenandoah.on.worldcat.org/oclc/464695264

Bandura, A. (1989). Human agency in social cognitive theory. *American Psychologist, 44*(9), 1175–1184. Retrieved from http://www.stiftelsen-hvasser.no/documents/Bandura_Human_Agency_in_social_Cognitiv_theory.pdf

Bandura, A. (1995). *Self-Efficacy in changing societies.* Cambridge: Cambridge University Press.

References 113

Beckhard, R. (2018, December). *Encyclopedia of management. Organizational development*. Retrieved from https://www.referenceforbusiness.com/management/Ob-Or/Organizational-Development.html

Benesch, S. (2017). *Considering emotions in critical English language teaching: Theories and praxis*. New York: Routledge Taylor & Francis.

Best College Reviews. (2018). The top 15 online TEFL certificate programs. Retrieved from https://www.bestcollegereviews.org/top/online-tefl-certificate-programs/

Better Health. (2012). Work-related stress. Retrieved from https://www.betterhealth.vic.gov.au/health/healthyliving/work-related-stress

Blackburn, J. (2015). *An evaluation of teacher morale in four elementary schools: The difference a school makes* (Dissertation). Retrieved from https://digitalcommons.nl.edu/diss/118/

Brown, A., Bimrose, J., Barnes, S-A., & Hughes, D. (2012). The role of career adaptabilities for mid-career changers. *Journal of Vocational Behavior, 80*, 754–761. https://doi.org/10.1016/j.jvb.2012.01.003

Brown, B. (2010, June). *The power of vulnerability* (video file). Retrieved from https://www.ted.com/talks/brene_brown_on_vulnerability?language=en

Canagarajah, A. S. (1999). Interrogating the "native speaker fallacy": Non-linguistic roots, non-pedagogical results. In G. Braine (Ed.), *Non-native educators in English language teaching* (pp. 77–92). Mahwah, NJ: Erlbaum.

Careers New Zealand. (2012). Donald Super developmental self-concept (PDF file). Retrieved from https://www.careers.govt.nz/assets/pages/docs/career-theory-model-super.pdf

Carkhuff, R. R., Alexik, M., & Anderson, S. (1967). Do we have a theory of vocational choice? *The Personnel and Guidance Journal, 46*(4), 335–345.

Carter, G. W., Cook, K. W., & Dorsey, D. W. (2009). *Career paths: Charting courses to success for organizations and their employees*. Sussex: Wiley-Blackwell Publishing.

Celep, C. (2000). The correlation of the factors: The prospective teacher's sense of efficacy and beliefs, and attitudes about student control (Abstract). *National FORUM of Teacher Educational Administration and Supervision Journal, 17E*(4). Retrieved from https://eric.ed.gov/?id=ED451157

Cheung, Y., Said, S., Park, K., & Werbińska, D. (2015). Advances and current trends in language teacher identity research. *System, 51*, 93–95. https://doi.org/10.1016/j.system.2015.04.006. Retrieved from https://shenandoah.on.worldcat.org/oclc/5821691338

Chism, M. (n.d.). *Career development theory* (video). Retrieved from https://study.com/academy/lesson/career-development-theories.html

Chism, M., & Relihan, T. (2019, May 6). *3 signs a conversation needs to happen*. Retrieved from https://www.smartbrief.com/original/2019/05/3-signs-conversation-needs-happen

Chubbuck, S. M., Clift, R. T., Allard, J., & Quinlan, J. (2001). Playing it safe as a novice teacher: Implications for programs for new teachers. *Journal of Teacher Education, 52*(5), 365–376.

Coombe, C., England, L., & Schmidt, J. (2012). *Reigniting, retooling, and retiring in English language teaching*. Ann Arbor, MI: University of Michigan Press. Retrieved from https://shenandoah.on.worldcat.org/oclc/741023752

114 References

Crane, B. (2015). For a more creative brain, travel! *Atlantic Monthly Magazine*. Retrieved from https://www.theatlantic.com/health/archive/2015/03/for-a-more-creative-brain-travel/388135/?utm_campaign=the-atlantic&utm_content=5c94a79e4b73850001c720 be_ta&utm_medium=social&utm

David, S. (2016). Emotional agility. *Get unstuck, embrace change and thrive in work and life*. New York: Penguin Random House.

David, S. (2018, March 25). *TED talk – Discomfort is the price of admission to a meaningful life* (video file). Rich Roll. Retrieved from https://www.youtube.com/watch?v=8B6e2ca2_qw&t=48s

Davis, L. C. (2015, August 31). When mindfulness meets the classroom. *The Atlantic Magazine*. Retrieved from https://www.theatlantic.com/education/archive/2015/08/mindfulness-education-schools-meditation/402469/

Day, C., & Gu, Q. (2010). *The new lives of teachers*. London, UK: Routledge https://doi.org/10.4324/9780203847909

Day, C., & Sachs, J. (2004). *International handbook on the continuing professional development of teachers*. Berkshire, England: Open University Press.

Decker, L., & Rimm-Kaufman, S. (2008). Personality characteristics and teacher beliefs among pre-service teachers. *Teacher Education Quarterly, 35*(2), 45–64. Retrieved from http://www.jstor.org/stable/23479223

Díaz-Maggioli, G. (2004). *Teacher-centered professional development*. Alexandria, VA: Association for Supervision and Curriculum Development. Retrieved from http://web.a.ebscohost.com/ehost/ebookviewer/ebook/bmxlYmtfXzExNDQ2NV9fQU41?sid=f8343d22-bf2f-491c-99bb-d53c1da8a0d4@sessionmgr4006&vid=8&format=EB&lpid=lp_1&rid=0

Dörnyei, Z. (2014). Motivation in second language learning. In M. Celce-Murcia, D. Brinton, M. A. Snow, & D. Bohlke (Eds.), *Teaching English as a second or foreign language* (4th ed.). Boston, MA: Cengage Learning.

Dörnyei, Z., & Ushioda, E. (2011). *Teaching and researching motivation* (2nd ed.). New York: Routledge Taylor & Francis.

Duberle, J., Carmichael, F., & Smzigin, I. (2013). Exploring women's retirement: Continuity, context and career transition. *Gender, Work and Organization, 21*(1), 71–90. https://doi.org/10.1111/gwao.12013

Eckert, J. (2016). *The novice advantage: Fearless practice for every teacher*. Thousand Oaks, CA: Corwin – A Sage Publication.

Edwards, E. A. (2003). *Retention and motivation of veteran teachers* (Electronic theses and dissertations, paper 742). Retrieved from http://dc.etsu.edu/etd/742

Eikhof, D. R., Warhurst, C., & Haunschild, A. (2007). Introduction: What work? What life? What balance? Critical reflections on the work-life balance debate. *Employee Relations, 29*(4), 325–339.

Elsheikh, A., Coombe, C., & Effiong, O. (2018). *The role of language teaching associations in professional development*. Cham, Switzerland: Springer. https://doi.org/10.1007/978-3-030-00967-0

Elton, C. (2009). *The carrot principle: How the best managers use their strengths to engage their people, retain talent and accelerate performance*. New York: Free Press.

Emerson, B. (2009). A manager's guide to coaching – Simple and effective ways to get the best out of your employees. *Development and Learning in Organizations: An International Journal, 3*(23). https://doi.org/10.1108/dlo.2009.08123cae.001

England, L. (2006). Methodology in Arabic language teacher education. *Handbook for Arabic Language Teaching Professionals in the 21st Century* (pp. 419–436). Abingdon, UK: Routledge.

England, L. (Ed.). (2012). *Online language teacher education: TESOL perspectives*. New York City, NY: Routledge Taylor-Francis Publishers.

England, L. (2018). Communities of practice. In J. I. Liontas (Ed.), *The TESOL encyclopedia of English language teaching* (Vol. 8). New York, NY: Wiley-Blackwell Publishers. doi. org/10.1002/9781118784235.eelt0396

Exchange Program. (n.d.). *English language fellow program*. Retrieved from https://exchanges. state.gov/us/program/english-language-fellow-program

Exchange Program. (n.d.). *English language specialist program*. Retrieved from https:// exchanges.state.gov/us/program/english-language-specialist-program

Falout, J., Murphey, T., & Stillwell, C. (2012). Avoiding burnout by lighting fires: Three contexts of change. In C. Coombe, L. England & J. R. Schmidt (Eds.), *Reigniting, retooling and retiring in English language teaching* (pp. 9–22). Ann Arbor: University of Michigan Press.

Farrell, T. S. C. (2008). Here's the book, go teach the class: ELT practicum support. *RELC Journal, 39*(2), 226–241. https://doi.org/10.1177/0033688208092186

Farrell, T. S. C. (2012). Novice-service language teacher development: Bridging the gap between preservice and in-service education and development. *TESOL Quarterly, 46*(3), 435–449. https://doi.org/10.1002/tesq.36

Fessler, R. (1985). *Career-long teacher education*. Springfield, IL: Charles C. Thomas.

Fisher, M. (2013). *Finding your career path without losing your mind: Emotional management for job seekers and career changers*. Scotts Valley, CA, US: CreateSpace Independent Publishing Platform (a division of Amazon).

Fowler, S. (2018). *How to generate positive energy* (weblog comment). Retrieved from https:// www.smartbrief.com/original/2018/10/how-generate-positive-energy

Freeman, D., Katz, A., Garcia Gomez, P., & Burns, A. (2015). English-for-teaching: Rethinking teacher proficiency in the classroom. *ELT Journal, 69*(2). https://doi. org/10.1093/elt/ccu074

Gardner, R. C., & Lambert, W. E. (1972). *Attitudes and motivation in second language learning*. Rowley, MA: Newbury House Publishers.

Gifford, J. (2007). Work-life balance. Retrieved from https://www.employment-studies. co.uk/system/files/resources/files/op13.pdf

Ginsberg, E., Ginsburg, S. W., Axelrad, S., & Herma, J. L. (1951). *Occupational choice: An approach to a general theory*. New York, NY: Columbia University Press.

Goleman, D. (1995). *Emotional intelligence*. New York: Bantam Books.

Graddol, D. (2006). *English next: Why global English may mean the end of "English as a foreign language"*. London: British Council. MLA (Modern Language Association).

Griffiths, V., Thompson, S., & Hryniewicz, L. (2014). Landmarks in the professional and academic development of mid-career teacher educators. *European Journal of Teacher Education, 37*(1), 74–90. https://doi.org/10.1080/02619768.2013.825241

Hall, E. T. (1959). *The silent language*. NY: Random House – Anchor Books.

Halliday, M. A. K. (1982). Linguistics and the teacher. In R. Carter (Ed.), *Linguistics and teacher education* (p. 13). New York: Routledge Publishers.

Harrison, C. H., & J. Killion. (2007). Ten roles for teacher leaders. *Educational Leadership, 65*(1). Retrieved from http://www.ascd.org/publications/educational-leadership/sept07/vol65/num01/Ten-Roles-for-Teacher-Leaders.aspx

116 References

Hastings, C. J. (2012). *Attitudes & acculturation: A qualitative case study of EFL teachers in Saudi Arabia [unpublished dissertation].* Memphis, TN: The University of Memphis.

Heath, T. (2018, July 20). How to quit your job. *Washington Post*, p. G3.

Hofstede, G. J. (2018). *Cultural comparison – Indonesia and the United States.* Retrieved from https://www.hofstede-insights.com/country-comparison/indonesia,the-usa/

Holland, J. L. (1987). Current status of Holland's theory of careers: Another perspective. *Career Development Quarterly, 36*(1), 24–30.

Holland, J. L. (1996). Exploring careers with a typology: What we have learned and some new directions. *American Psychologist, 51*(4), 397–406. http://dx.doi.org/10.1037/0003-066X.51.4.397

Holland, N. N. (1990). *Holland's guide to psychoanalytic psychology and literature-and-psychology.* New York: Oxford University Press. http://web.b.ebscohost.com/ehost/detail/detail?vid =0&sid=0e4f880d-d1cf-4a92-ac84-5856472f870e%40sessionmgr101&bdata=JkF1dGhUeX BlPWlwLHVybCxjb29raWUmc2l0ZT1laG9zdC1saXZl#AN=292767&db=nlebk

Huberman, M. A. (1993). *The Lives of Teachers.* New York: Teachers College Press. *International House Journal of Education and Development.* Retrieved from http://ihjournal. com/teachers-professional-life-cycles

IATEFL (2018). IATEFL's mission, goals and practices. Retrieved from https://members. iatefl.org/downloads/member_info/IATEFL_mission_goals_practices.pdf

IGI Global: Disseminator of Knowledge. (n.d.). *What is a novice teacher.* Retrieved from https://www.igi-global.com/dictionary/teacher-fellows/51329.

Ingersoll, R., Merrill, L., & Stuckey, D. (2014). *Seven trends: The transformation of the teaching force* (CPRE Research Reports). Retrieved from https://repository.upenn.edu/cpre_ researchreports/79 and http://www.cpre.org/sites/default/files/workingpapers/1506_ 7trendsapril2014.pdf

Institute for Employment Studies. (2007). Annual review (PDF file). Retrieved from https:// www.employment-studies.co.uk/system/files/resources/files/annrev07.pdf

Johanns, K. (2018, December 30). How successful people write their self-reviews. *The Washington Post.* Retrieved from https://www.pressreader.com/usa/the-washington-post.../20181230/283085595307359

Johnson, B. (2019). *Putting teachers first. How to inspire, motivate and connect with your staff.* New York: Routledge Taylor & Francis.

Johnson, S. M., & Birkeland, S. E. (2003). Pursuing a "sense of success": New teachers explain their career decisions. *American Educational Research Journal, 40*(3), 581–617. https://doi. org/10.3102/00028312040003581

Jones, B. B., & Brazzel, M. (2014). *NTL Institute handbook of organizational development and change: Principles, practices and perspectives* (2nd ed.). San Francisco, CA: Wiley Publishers, on behalf of NTL.

Kahn, D. L., & Katz, D. (1952). *Leadership practices in relation to productivity.* Ann Arbor, MI: The University of Michigan Social Research Center.

Karnitz, K. (2019, February 14). *Opinion: Teachers aren't losers.* Retrieved from https://www. pbs.org/newshour/education/opinion-teachers-arent-losers-theyre-lifesavers

Kirk, J., & Wall, C. (2010). Resilience and loss in work identities: A narrative analysis of some retired teachers' work-life histories. *British Educational Research Journal, 36*(4), 627–641. Retrieved from https://www.jstor.org/stable/27823636

Klassen, R. M., & Chiu, M. M. (2011). The occupational commitment and intention to quit of practicing and pre-service teachers: Influence of self-efficacy, job stress, and teaching context. *Contemporary Educational Psychology, 36*(2), 114–129.

Retrieved from https://ac.els-cdn.com/S0361476X11000038/1-s2.0-S0361476X11000038-main.pdf?_tid=230b042a-baaf-4dc8-8a8a-378eadbcf144&acdnat=1544717694_b231a3ec4bd965ba09aba7d0793b5a27

Kubanyiova, M. (2009). Possible selves in language teacher development. In E. Ushioda & Z. Dörnyei (Eds.), *Motivation, language identity and the L2 self* (pp. 314–332). Bristol, UK: Multilingual Matters.

Kubota, R., & Sun, Y. (2012). *Demystifying career paths after graduate school: A guide for second language professionals in higher education (Contemporary language studies series)*. Charlotte, NC: IAP – Information Age Publishing. Retrieved from https://shenandoah.on.worldcat.org/oclc/819631519

Kucharvy, T. (2014). *Creating a pathway to your dream career: Designing and controlling a career around your life goals* (1st ed.). New York, NY: Business Expert Press. https://www.springer.com/us/book/9783030009663

Leong, F. L. (Ed.). (2008). *Encyclopedia of Counseling*. Los Angeles, CA: SAGE. http://dx.doi.org/10.4135/9781412963978

Loehr, A. (n.d.). *Generational diversity guru*. Retrieved from https://www.anneloehr.com/about-anne-loehr/

Ludlow, C., & Kent, R. (2011). *Building a research career*. San Diego, CA: Plural Pub. Retrieved from https://shenandoah.on.worldcat.org/oclc/865509047

Mahboob, A., & England, L. (2018). Reality and potential: English language teacher associations in the 21st century. In A. Elsheikh, C. Coombe, & O. Effiong (Eds.), *The role of language teacher associations in professional development* (pp. 25–38). New York: Springer. Retrieved from https://www.springer.com/us/book/9783030009663

Mana, M., & England, L. (2017). Proposing professional standards for Arabic teacher certification. In K. Wahba, L. England, & Z. Taha (Eds.), *Handbook for Arabic language teaching professionals in the 21st century* (Chapter 25) (pp. 25–38). New York: Routledge Taylor & Francis.

Marcus, B. (2015). *The politics of promotion: How high-achieving women get ahead and stay ahead*. Hoboken, NJ: Wiley. Retrieved from https://shenandoah.on.worldcat.org/oclc/902986781

Margulies, N., & Raia, A. P. (1972). *Organizational development: Values, process, and technology*. New York, NY: McGraw-Hill Book Company.

Megyeri, K. A. (1996). Tribute. *English Journal*, 85, 24–29.

Minor, L. C., Onwuegbuzie, A. J., Witcher, A. E., & James, T. L. (2002). Preservice teachers' educational beliefs and their perceptions of characteristics of effective teachers. *The Journal of Educational Research*, *96*, 116–127.

Moss, G. (2016). Knowledge, education and research: Making common cause across communities of practice. *British Educational Research Journal*, *42*(6), 927–944. https://doi.org/10.1002/berj.3249

Newman, K. S. (2019). *Downhill from here: Retirement insecurity in the age of inequality*. New York, NY: Metropolitan Books.

Nicholson, N. (2018, October 10). What's the point of purpose? London Business School Review. Retrieved from https://www.london.edu/faculty-and-research/lbsr/whats-the-point-of-purpose

Osipow, S. H. (1973). *Theories of career development*. New York, NY: Appleton-Century-Crofts.

Pennington, M. C. (1989). Directions for faculty evaluation in language education. *Language, Culture and Curriculum*, *2*(3), 167. https://doi.org/10.1080/0790831890952506420

118 References

Pennsylvania State Department of Education, K-12. 2018 Career ready PA. Retrieved from https://www.education.pa.gov/K-12/CareerReadyPA/Pages/default.aspx

Perschel, A. (2018, October 18). *How to power pause under stress.* Retrieved from https://germaneconsulting.com/leaders-power-pause-under-stress/

Poelmans, S. (2005). Work and family. *An international research perspective.* Series in applied psychology. Mahwah, NJ: Lawrence Erlbaum Associates. Retrieved from https://shenandoah.on.worldcat.org/oclc/58730890

Powers, C. (2019, March 15). Presentation at TESOL International Association Convention Annual Business Meeting, Atlanta, GA.

Prior, R. (2019, May 27). *Burnout is an official medical diagnosis, World Health Organization says.* Retrieved from https://www.cnn.com/2019/05/27/health/who-burnout-disease-trnd/index.html?no-st=1559226612

Public Broadcasting System. (2019, February 14). Opinion: Teachers aren't losers. They're lifesavers. Retrieved from https://www.pbs.org/newshour/education/opinion-teachers-arent-losers-theyre-lifesavers

Pultorak, E. G. (1996). Following the developmental process of reflection in novice teachers: Three years of investigation. *Journal of Teacher Education, 47*(4), 283–291. https://doi.org/10.1177/0022487196474006

Quy, L. (2018, October 17). *Why success alone doesn't mean you've made real progress* (web log comment). Retrieved from https://www.smartbrief.com/original/2018/10/why-success-alone-doesnt-mean-youve-made-real-progress?utm_source=brief

Radford, C. P. (2017). *Mentoring in action: Guiding, sharing and reflecting with novice teachers.* Thousand Oaks, CA. Corwin – A Sage Company.

Richards, J. C., & Rodgers, T. (1982), Method: Approach, design, and procedure. *TESOL Quarterly, 16*, 153–168. https://doi.org/10.2307/3586789

Richardson, S., & Maggioli, G. D. (2018). *Effective professional development: Principles and best practices.* Cambridge Papers in ELT. Cambridge, UK: Cambridge University Press.

Richter, D., Kunter, M., Klusmann, U., Ludtke, O., & Baumert, J. (2011). Professional development across the teaching career: Teachers' uptake of formal and informal learning opportunities. *Teaching and Teacher Education, 27*(1), 116–126. https://doi.org/10.1002/tesq.36

Rogers, E. M., Hart, W. B., & Miike, Y. (2002). Edward T. Hall and the history of intercultural communication: The United States and Japan. *Keio Communication Review, 24*(1–5). Retrieved from http://www.mediacom.keio.ac.jp/publication/pdf2002/review24/2.pdf

Salas Serrano, L. A., Schrader, U., & Gomez, K. Leadership emergence within MEXTESOL. In A. Elsheikh, C. Coombe, & O. Effiong (Eds.), *The Role of Language Teacher Associations in Professional Development.* Second language learning and teaching (pp. 201–214). New York: Springer. https://doi.org/10.1007/978-3-030-00967-0_15201

Span, P. (2018, July 6). He called older colleagues "dead wood." Two sued for age discrimination. *The New York Times.* Retrieved from https://www.nytimes.com/2018/07/06/health/age-discrimination-ohio-state.html

Sridhar, S. (1993). What is applied linguistics? *International Journal of Applied Linguistics, 3*(1), 3–16. https://doi.org/10.1111/j.1473-4192.1993.tb00040.x

Steffy, B. E., & Wolfe, M. P. (2001). A life-cycle model for career teachers. *Kappa Delta Pi Record, 38*(1), 16–19. https://doi.org/10.1080/00228958.2001.10518508

Steffy, B. E., Wolfe, M. P., Pasch, S. H., & Enz, B. J. (2000). *Life cycle of the career teacher.* Thousand Oaks, CA: Corwin Press, Inc.

References   119

Super, D. E. (1973). Super's developmental self-concept theory of vocational behavior. In S.H. Osipow (Ed.), *Theories of career development* (pp. 131–172). New York, NY: Appleton-Century-Crofts.

Super, D. E. (1980). A life-span, life-space approach to career development. *Journal of Vocational Behavior, 16*(3), 282–298.

Sylvia, R. D., & Hutchison, T. (1985). What makes Ms. Johnson teach? A study of teacher motivation. *Human Relations, 38*. https://doi.org/10.1177/001872678503800902

Tait, M. (2008). Resilience as a contributor to novice teacher success, commitment, and retention. *Teacher Education Quarterly, 35*(4), 57–75.

Tannacito, D. (2013). *What, me? An administrator? English language teachers as program administrators.* Alexandria, VA: TESOL Publications.

Tedick, D. J. (2005). *Second language teacher education: International perspectives.* Mahwah, NJ: Routledge.

TESOL International Association. (n.d.). Mission and values. Retrieved from https://www.tesol.org/about-tesol/association-governance/mission-and-values

TESOL International Association. (2017, February 10, 11). Summit on the future of the TESOL profession, Athens Greece. Retrieved from https://www.tesol.org/summit-2017

TESOL International Association. (n.d.). *TESOL leadership certificate program.* Retrieved from https://sites.tesol.org/MemberPortal/Events/2018/PL18_LDCP/TESOL-Event-Detail?EventKey=PL18_LDCP

Thomson, P. (1992). *Shakespeare's professional career.* Cambridge, England: Cambridge University Press. Retrieved from https://shenandoah.on.worldcat.org/oclc/24174208

Thoonen, E. J., Sleegers, P. J. C., Oort, F. J., Peetsma, T. D., & Geijsel, F. P. (2011). How to improve teaching practices: The role of teacher motivation, organizational factors, and leadership practices. *Educational Administration Quarterly, 47*(3), 496–536. https://doi.org/10.1177/0013161X11400185

Umbach, P. D., & Wawrzynski, M. R. (2005). Faculty do matter: The role of college faculty in student learning and engagement. *Research in Higher Education, 46*(2), 153–184. https://doi.org/10.1007/s11162-004-1598-1

Ushioda, E. (2003). Motivation as a socially mediated process. In D. Little, J. Ridley, & E. Ushioda (Eds.), *Learner autonomy in the foreign language classroom: Teacher, learner, curriculum and assessment.* Dublin, Ireland: Authentik Language Learning Resources Ltd. Retrieved from https://www.researchgate.net/profile/David_Little2/publication/317264706_Learner_autonomy_in_the_foreign_language_classroom_teacher_learner_curriculum_and_assssment/links/592ed1eea6fdcc89e76992c0/Learner-autonomy-in-the-foreign-language-classroom-teacher-learner-curriculum-and-assssment.pdf#page=98

Ushioda, E., & Dörnyei, Z. (2009). *Motivation, language identity and the L2 self.* Bristol, UK: Multilingual Matters. Retrieved from http://search.ebscohost.com/login.aspx?direct=true&db=nlebk&AN=245456&site=bsi-live

van Harmelan, M. (2006). *Personal learning environments.* International Conference on Advanced Learning Technologies. Retrieved August from https://pdfs.semanticscholar.org/3a80/0f41a3431cd05b37e882c34dc434aa27bbf3.pdf

Wahba, K., England, L., & Taha, Z. (2017). *Handbook for Arabic language teaching professionals in the 21st century* (Vol. II). New York: Routledge Taylor & Francis. https://doi.org/10.4324/9781315676111

120 References

Wahba, K., Taha, Z., & England, L. (2012). *Handbook for Arabic language teaching professionals in the 21st century* (1st ed.). New York: Lawrence Erlbaum. https://doi.org/10.4324/9780203824757

Walls, R. T., Nardi, A. H., & Von Minden, A. M. (2002). The characteristics of effective and ineffective teachers. *Teacher Education Quarterly, 29*(1), 39–48. Retrieved from http://suproxy.su.edu/login?url=http://search.ebscohost.com/login.aspx?direct=true&AuthType=ip,url,cookie&db=ofm&AN=507795834&site=ehost-live

Watkins, C. E., Jr., Bradford, B., Lew, D. E., & Himmel, C. D. (1986). Major contributors and major contributions to the vocational behavior literature. *Journal of Vocational Behavior, 28*(1), 42–47. Retrieved from https://www.sciencedirect.com/science/article/abs/pii/0001879186900382

Watt, H. M. G., Richardson, P. W., & Smith, K. (Eds.). (2017). *Global perspectives on teacher motivation*. Cambridge, England: Cambridge University Press.

West, C. P., Dyrbye, L. N., Erwin, P. J., & Shanafelt, T. D. (2016). Interventions to prevent and reduce physician burnout: A systematic review and meta-analysis. *The Lancet, 388*(10057), 2272–2281.

White, M., Hill, S., McGovern, P., Mills, C., & Smeaton, D. (2003). High performance management practices, working hours and work-life balance. *BJIR: An International Journal of Employment Relations, 41*(2), 75–195. https://doi.org/10.1111/1467-8543.00268

Wikipedia. (n.d.). Applied linguistics. Retrieved from https://en.wikipedia.org/wiki/Applied_linguistics

Wikipedia. (n.d.). Terminal degree. Retrieved from https://en.wikipedia.org/wiki/Terminal_degree

Wilson, E., & Deaney, R. (2010). Changing career and changing identity: How do teacher career changers exercise agency in identity construction? *Social Psychology of Education, 13*(2), 169–183. https://doi.org/10.1007/s11218-010-9119-x

Winkler, E. (2019, June). Was Shakespeare a woman? *Atlantic Magazine*. Retrieved from https://www.theatlantic.com/magazine/archive/2019/06/who-is-shakespeare-emilia-bassano/588076/?utm_source=facebook&utm_campaign=the-atlantic-fb-test-961-1-&utm_content=edit-promo&utm_medium=social

Wiseman, D. L. (2012). The intersection of policy, reform and teacher education. *Journal of Teacher Education, 63*(2), 87–91.

Yeatts, D., Folts, E., & Knapp, J. (2000). Older workers adaptation to a changing workplace: Employment issues for the 21st century. *Educational Gerontology, 26*(6), 565–582. https://doi.org/10.1080/03601270050133900

INDEX

Note: *Italicized* page numbers refer to figures, **bold** page numbers refer to tables.

10 roles of teacher leaders (Harrison and Killion) 61

academic programs 30–31, 35, 52
academic research 16
accommodators 7
acupuncture treatments 80
Adoniou, Misty 66
advocacy 106–108; career stages and **109**; defined 108; intentional focus on 107–108; as top priority for professionals 107
Afghanistan 90
age differences 96–97
Alzheimer's disease 87
American Association of Applied Linguistics 63
American University in Cairo (AUC) 89–90
Amzat, I. H. 62
anxiety 3, 70
appetite loss 80
applied linguistics 13, 34–36
appreciation 83, 84; *see also* rewards
ASCD *see* Association for Supervision and Curriculum Development (ASCD)
Ashforth, B. E. 47–48

assessment challenges 96
Association for Supervision and Curriculum Development (ASCD) 19, 61–62
The Atlantic Magazine 74
attitudes 21, 44, 45; English teachers **25–26**; negative 69
audits 52
Augier, M. 50

bad boss 72
Bahasa Indonesia 91
Bahawalpur 90
balance/imbalance 72–76, 80; *see also* life balance
Bandura, A. 16
Better Health 70
Blackburn, J. 73
body 74, **77**, 80
boss 72
Brazzel, M. 52
Brown, B. 66
burnout 67, 74, 76, 80, 84, 92, **109**
Burns, A. 98
business imperatives 20

Cairo 89–90
Canagarajah, A. S. 98
CARE *see* Cultivating Awareness and Resilience in Education (CARE)

122 Index

career path 64–66, 70, 79; organizational development 55–58; phases 64
career path development (CPD) 1–3, 6, 9, 11–27, 60, 84; academic research 16; attitudes 21; career trends 22, **25–26**; context of *14*; efficacy/skills in 22; leadership and *15*, 18–19; life balance *15*, 20; organizational development *15*, 18; overview 12–14; professional identity/motivation in 21; rationale for theoretical approach 16–17; stages *15*, 15–16, 22–24; teacher education *15*, 17; teacher motivation *15*, 17–18, 42; theoretical model 20–24
career skills 106
career trends 22, **25–26**
career typology 16
Carter, G. W. 1–2
challenges: address 91; assessment 96; career 11; life balance 20; opportunities and 7; professional 85; professional development 8; professional lives 12; work-related 22, 75
changes: demographic 20; identity 81; life 69–70; personal 69
churches 102
cognitive skills 74
Colombian students 35
commitment 4, 5, 7, **25–26**, 43, 51, 54, 73, 84, 95, 100
communication *see* cross-cultural communication
Communities of Practice 45
community-based organizations 102
concerns 3, **26**, 38, 78, 96, 100
continuing professional development 6
contract 87
Cook, K. W. 1–2
Coombe, C. 54–55
CPD *see* career path development (CPD)
criticism 3
cross-cultural communication 13, 36–38
Cultivating Awareness and Resilience in Education (CARE) 75
Czech Republic 90

Davis, Lauren Cassani 74–75
Day, Cathy 5, 33
dementia 87
demographic changes 20
departmental identity 18
depression 70, 73, 80

Descriptive Linguistics 32
disappointments 3
doctoral degree 31, 32, 89
Dörnyei, Z. 7, 17, 43–45
Dorsey, D. W. 1–2
downsizing 3, 58
D. Scott Enright Service Award 88

Educational Leadership (magazine) 19
efficacy 22; English teachers **25–26**
Effiong, O. 54–55
EFL *see* English as a Foreign Language (EFL)
Eikhof, D. R. 70
ELF *see* English Language Fellows (ELF)
Elsheikh, A. 54–55
EL Spec *see* English Language Specialist (EL Spec)
Elton, C. 83
emotional intelligence 71, 79
emotional labor 48
emotions 3
Employee Relations 70
employment 98
Encyclopedia of Management (Augier and Teece) 50
England, L. 31, 45, 90, 110, 111
English as a Foreign Language (EFL) 15, 24, 46, 67
English as a Second Language (ESL) 15, 31–33, 103–105; classes 35; English teachers 25; mid-career/career switchers teachers 46; program alumni 66; semi-retired teachers 24; teacher educator 39; teaching career 35; teaching staff 67
English for some or another Specific Purpose (ESP) 30
English for young learners (EYL) 30
English Language Fellows (ELF) 90, 91–92
English Language Specialist (EL Spec) 90–91
English teachers 4, 6, 19, 38, 55, 91, 98, 102; attitudes **25–26**; career trends 22, **25–26**; efficacy **25–26**; English as a Second Language (ESL) **25**; identity **25–26**; life balance at career stages **77**; motivation **25–26**; skills **25–26**, 100; *see also* teacher(s)
esketamine 80
ESL *see* English as a Second Language (ESL)
ESP *see* English for some or another Specific Purpose (ESP)
EYL *see* English for young learners (EYL)

Index **123**

failures 3, 94
fake news 51
family demands 73–74
fear 3, 9, **77**
feelings of worthlessness 80
Fessler, R. 2
Folts, E. 78
Forbes Magazine 78
forced leadership training 62–63
formal rewards 83; *see also* rewards
Fowler, Susan 47
Freeman, D. 98

Garcia Gomez, P. 98
Gardner, R. C. 43
geographically mobile 85
Georgetown University 90
Ginsburg, S. W. 16
Gomez, Cathy 64–66
Google 12
government policy 20

Hall, Edward T. 37
Halliday, M. A. K. 35
Harrison, C. H. 19, 61
Hastings, Chris 44
Haunschild, A. 70
Hofstede, Gerte 37–38
Holland, J. L. 16
Hong Kong Airport 86
Huberman, M. A. 2
Humphrey, R. H. 47–48
hyphenated linguistics 34–35

IATEFL *see* International Association
    of Teachers of English as a Foreign
    Language (IATEFL)
identity 3; change 81; departmental 18;
    English teachers **25–26**; institutional
    18; professional 21, 84; students 12;
    teachers 12
IEP *see* Intensive English
    Program (IEP)
imbalance *see* balance/imbalance
Indonesia 91
informal rewards 83; *see also* rewards
informal training 63
Ingersoll, R. 70
inhalants 80
inner circles 84
Institute for Employment Studies 20
institutional identity 18

institutional support: mid-career/career
    switchers 95–96; novice/beginners
    teachers 95; preservice teachers 95;
    semiretired teachers 96–97; veteran
    teachers 96; *see also* workplace teacher
    support
instructional technology 58
Intensive English Program (IEP) 36,
    50, 86
Intentional TESOL Career Path
    Development 94–95, 104–111
internal audits 52
International Association of Teachers
    of English as a Foreign Language
    (IATEFL) 2, 53, 54–55
*International Handbook on the Continuing
    Professional Development of Teachers* (Day
    and Sachs) 5
International Phonetic Alphabet (IPA)
    35–36
Internet 19, 74
intrinsic motivation 46
IPA *see* International Phonetic
    Alphabet (IPA)
Iranian students 35
Islamabad 90

job insecurity 70
job loss 85
job options 1
job performance 79
job promotion 63–64, 85
job-related stress 70, 74
job responsibilities 70
job satisfaction 1, 16, 18, 67, 75
job security 7, 44, 46, 51
Johanns, K. 79
Johnson, B. 79, 83
Jones, B. B. 52

Karachi, Islamabad 91
Katz, A. 98
Killion, J. 19, 61
Knapp, J. 78
knowledge 1; leadership **65**; skills
    and 23, 35–40, 45–46, 52, 57–58, 63,
    65, 90, 108
Kubanyiova, M. 17

labor *see* emotional labor
Lahore 91
Lambert, W. E. 43

124 Index

language pedagogy 36
Language Teaching Associations (LTAs) 97, 98; mid-career/career switchers and 99–100; novice/beginners teachers and 99; preservice teachers and 98; semiretired teachers and 101; veteran teachers and 100
LDCP *see* Leadership Development Certificate Program (LDCP)
leadership 60–67; career path 64–66; career path development and *15*, 18–19; development **65**; forced leadership training 62–63; job promotion 63–64; mid-career/career switcher teachers **65**; novice/beginners teachers **65**; overview 60–61; personal narrative 62–66; preservice teachers **65**; recommendations 66–67; semiretired teachers **65**; teacher leadership 61–66
Leadership Development Certificate Program (LDCP) 62
life balance 69–81; balance/imbalance 72–76, 80; body and 80–81; career path development (CPD) *15*, 20; career stages **77**; challenges 20; coping with imbalance 80; factors 79; mid-career/ career switcher teachers **77**; novice/ beginners teachers **77**; overview 69–70; personal narrative 71–72; preservice teachers **77**; recommendations 76–81; semiretired teachers **77**; soul and 81; tips 79–80; veteran teachers **77**
life changes 69–70
lifestyles 1
linguistics 13, 32, 34–36
Loehr, Anne 66–67
loyalty 51
LTA *see* Language Teaching Associations (LTAs)

MacArthur Foundation Grants 63
Maclay, Howard 35
Malaysia 91
Margulies, N. 52
massive open online courses (MOOC) 102
material concerns 96
meditation 74
Merrill, L. 70
mid-career/career switchers 6, 15, 23, 46; advocacy skills **109**; characteristics **25**; English as a Second Language (ESL) 46; institutional support 95–96;

leadership **65**; life balance **77**; LTAs and 99–100
Middle East 91
milestones 85–92
mind 74, **77**, 80–81
mindfulness 74–75
Mindful Schools 75
mission statement, IATEFL 54
motivation 21; English teachers **25–26**; intrinsic 46; student 21; *see also* teacher motivation
Motivation, Language Identity and the L2 Self (Ushioda and Dörnyei) 17

National Endowment for the Humanities awards 63
needs 1; of employees 1; professional development 8; of schools 1; teachers' 6; training and development of teachers 4
negative relationships 81
networking 106
niche markets 30, 46
Nicholson, N. 46
non-governmental organizations 102
non-native English-speaking teachers (NNEST) 98
novice/beginner teachers 6, 15, 22–23, 46, 95–96; advocacy skills **109**; characteristics of **25**; institutional support 95; leadership **65**; life balance **77**; LTAs and 98–99; motivation 47

older workers 78
ongoing, systematic processes 57
online communications skills 110
Online Language Teacher Education – TESOL Perspectives (England) 109–110
on-the-job training 63
organizational development 50–58; career path development and *15*, 18; career paths 55–58; defined 50; IATEFL 53, 54–55; personal narrative 50–51; successes and shortcomings 51–54
organizational structure 56
Osipow, S. H 13–14, 16
ought-to selves 17

Pakistan 90
pedagogy 13
Pennington, Martha 44
Pennsylvania State Department of Education 12

Index **125**

personal changes 69
personal concerns **26**, 100
personality 18
Peshawar, Lahore 90
physical exercise 74
Pilates 80
places of employment 56–58
PLN *see* Professional Learning
    Networks (PLN)
possible self 17
Powers, Christopher 53, 98
preservice teachers 6, 15, 22, 97–98;
    advocacy skills **109**; characteristics
    of **25**; family obligations affecting
    73; graduate-level teacher education
    program 56; institutional support for
    95; leadership **65**; life balance **77**; LTAs
    and 98; motivation 45–46; *see also*
    teacher(s)
private club 32
problem-solving skills 74
professional associations 53–58, 84,
    97–103; *see also* Language Teaching
    Associations (LTAs)
professional development 5, 6, 55;
    challenges 8; goals 84; needs 8;
    opportunities 101–103; programs 52
professional identity 21, 84
professionalism 1
Professional Learning Networks (PLN)
    38–39
professional satisfaction 4, 11, 43
professional skills 5, 23, 36, 45, 62,
    110, 111
program alumni 66
promotions 3, 50
public schooling 30
Putting Teachers First: How To Inspire,
    Motivate and Connect with Your Staff
    (Johnson) 79, 83

Quy, L. 47

Raia, A. P. 52
recognition *see* rewards
rejection 3
relationships *see* negative relationships
research skills 46
responsibilities 2
rewards 83–85, 88–89, 92
Richards, J. C. 36
Rodgers, T. 36

The Role of Language Teacher Associations
    in Professional Development (Elsheikh,
    Coombe, and Effiong) 54–55

Sachs, J. 5
satisfaction *see* job satisfaction
Second Language Acquisition and
    Teacher Education (SLATE) 33–34
self-assessment 76, 79
self-care 20, 45, 71, 74, 92, 105, 107, 110
self-concept 16
self-doubt 3
self-esteem 3, 88
self-image 3
semiretired teachers 6, 15, 24, 46;
    advocacy skills **109**; characteristics
    of **26**; English as a Second Language
    (ESL) 24; institutional support 96–97;
    leadership **65**; life balance **77**; LTAs
    and 100–101
Shakespeare, William 6–7
Shenandoah University 91
Shrestha, Meera 81
skills 1, 3, 22; advocacy 106–108, **109**;
    career 106; cognitive 74; cross-cultural
    communication 37; English teachers
    25–26, 100; instructional technology
    58; knowledge and 23, 35–40, 45–46,
    52, 57–58, 63, **65**, 90, 108; leadership
    61, 63, 64, **65**; networking 106; online
    communications 110; problem-solving
    74; professional 5, 23, 36, 45, 62,
    110, 111; research 46; technology 58,
    108–111
Skype 19
SLATE *see* Second Language Acquisition
    and Teacher Education (SLATE)
sleeping difficulties 70
sleep loss 80
socialization 12
social media 19, 84, 102–103, 105
Society for Pakistani English Teachers
    (SPELT) 91
soul 74, **77**, 80, 81
South Sulawesi 91
SPELT *see* Society for Pakistani English
    Teachers (SPELT)
Sridhar, S. 34–35
Steffy, B. E. 2–3
stop-drop-relax strategy 80
stress *see* job-related stress; work-related
    stress

126 Index

Stuckey, D. 70
student debt 87
student motivation 21
success 1, 3, 11; professional 47
Super, D. E. 16, 56
supervisors 95

talent management 3
teacher(s): behaviors and habits 45;
   compensation 3; needs 6; personal note
   104–106; professional development
   opportunities 5, 101–103; role 4;
   see also English teachers; *specific entries*
teacher development 20–24
teacher education 30–41; applied
   linguistics 34–36; career path
   development and *15*, 17; cross-cultural
   communication 36–38; language
   pedagogy 36; next steps 38–40;
   overview 30–31; personal narrative
   31–34; programs 45; recommendations
   40–41
teacher leadership 61–66
teacher motivation 42–48; career path
   development and *15*, 17–18, 21; defined
   21; described 43–46; factors 17; next
   steps 47; overview 42–43; personal
   narrative 43; recommendations 47–48;
   see also motivation
Teacher of the Year 84
Teachers of English to Speakers of Other
   Languages (TESOL) 1–2; teacher
   education 17
teaching career 35
technology 58, 108–111
Teece, D. J. 50
tenure decisions 3
terminal degree 17, 31, 97
*The TESOL Encyclopedia of English
   Language Teaching* 45, 106
TESOL International Association 54, 97
Thailand 91
theoretical linguistics 32
theories 13–14
Theories of Career Development (Osipow)
   13–14
Thomson, Peter 6–7

too long work hours 73
Top 15 TEFL Certificate Programs
   (website) 30
top earners 46
trainer of trainer 63
training: forced leadership 62–63;
   informal 63; needs and development of
   teachers 4; on-the-job 63

UIUC *see* University of Illinois
   Champaign-Urbana (UIUC)
unappreciated work 73
United States Department of Education 75
United States Department of State 90
University of Illinois Champaign-Urbana
   (UIUC) 33
Ushioda, E. 7, 17, 21, 43–45

Valdez, N. P. 62
values 1, 3; norms and 14; theory and 14
veteran teachers 6, 15, 24, 58, 96;
   advocacy skills **109**; characteristics of
   26; institutional support 96; leadership
   65; life balance **77**; LTAs and 100;
   motivation 46

Warhurst, C. 70
The Washington Post 66–67, 79
What are applied linguistics? (Sridhar)
   34–35
WHO *see* World Health Organization
   (WHO)
Wolfe, M. P. 2–3
work environment 18
work ethic 4
work hours 73
work-life balance 70, 76
work performance 70
workplace teacher support 95;
   see also institutional support
work-related challenges 75
work-related stress 72–73
work satisfaction *see* job satisfaction
World Health Organization (WHO) 74

Yeatts, D. 78
yoga 74, 80